MY DAD HAD ONE OF THOSE

Giles Chapman and Richard Porter

BOOKS

CONTENTS

1 TYPICAL DAD

FORD ESCORT MK 1/2 10
MORRIS MARINA 14
AUSTIN 1100 16
HILLMAN AVENGER 18
VAUXHALL VIVA 20
AUSTIN ALLEGRO 22
HILLMAN HUNTER 24

2 SENSIBLE DAD

DATSUN SUNNY 28
VOLKSWAGEN GOLF 30
TOYOTA COROLLA 32
AUSTIN MAXI 34

3 EXECUTIVE DAD

TRIUMPH 2000 38
FORD GRANADA 40
ROVER SD1 42
FORD ZEPHYR/ZODIAC 44
VAUXHALL VICTOR 46
ROVER 2000 48

4 COMPACT DAD

MINI CLUBMAN ESTATE 52
VAUXHALL CHEVETTE 54
AUSTIN METRO 56
HILLMAN IMP 58
FORD ANGLIA 105E 60

5 LUXURY DAD

BMW 5-SERIES 64
MERCEDES-BENZ 200 66
JAGUAR XJ6 68
RANGE ROVER 70
TRIUMPH DOLOMITE 72

6 DEMOB DAD

AUSTIN CAMBRIDGE 76
STANDARD VANGUARD 78
VAUXHALL CRESTA/VELOX 80
FORD POPULAR/PREFECT 82
ROVER P4 84

7 '80s DAD
FORD SIERRA 88
AUSTIN MONTEGO 90
RENAULT 18 92
FORD ESCORT MK 3 94
VAUXHALL CAVALIER MK 2 96

8 FRUGAL DAD
CITROËN 2CV 100
LADA 102
RELIANT ROBIN 104
RENAULT 4 106
MINI 108

9 SPORTY DAD
OPEL MANTA 114
FORD CAPRI 116
RELIANT SCIMITAR GTE 120
TRIUMPH STAG 122

10 PRACTICAL DAD
PEUGEOT 504 ESTATE 126
VOLVO 245 128
LAND-ROVER 130
FORD TRANSIT 132
TOYOTA SPACE CRUISER 134

11 TECHNO DAD
CITROËN DS 138
AUSTIN PRINCESS 140
NSU RO80 142
AUDI 100 144
CITROËN GS 146

12 CORTINA DAD
FORD CORTINA MK 1 150
FORD CORTINA MK 2 152
FORD CORTINA MK 3 154
FORD CORTINA MK 4/5 156

Welcome to *My Dad Had One Of Those*, a gentle canter through some of the greatest cars ever to grace your father's driveway. When we were putting together this book we decided that it should cover a very specific era, starting in the late-1950s, when more and more Dads could afford a car for the first time, and ending sometime in the 1980s, when cars became the close relatives of the things we drive today and the nostalgia runs out.

Arriving at the 60 cars featured here wasn't easy. We looked at sales figures, we read contemporary road tests, we even thought about forming a panel of Dads to decide for us. But in the end we just went to the pub and picked a list of stuff we quite liked.

They may not have been the best cars ever, but they're certainly some of the best loved. They were sensible or practical or unusual or funny, or sometimes all of those things at once. And that made them rather like your Dad himself.

⫴TYPICAL DAD
Pure, honest, simple Dadness.

FORD ESCORT MK 1/2

(1967–1980)

The Ford Anglia 105E really worked for Ford, combining meat-pie engineering with a spicy body to make an affordable but nice-looking car that sold well. So when it came to replacing it, why monkey with the formula? Cost-effective chassis as complex as a potato? Moderate engines, just powerful, economical and reliable enough to avoid looking silly next to rival cars? Yep. Whole lot dressed up in a good-looking body that used trendy design ideas of the day from more glamorous American cars? Go on, then. And then garnish the well-tried formula with a new name so that it feels fresh and modern? Bingo.

Welcome to the Ford Escort. Nothing clever, nothing adventurous, but still as effective as a bow and arrow. Not just effective at seducing Dad into buying one, either, because the Mk 1 Escort was a mighty weapon in rallying too, which gave it an exciting edge of motor-sport glory, complemented by road-going versions of the mud-splattered racers – the RS1600, RS2000 and the oddly badged Mexico, given that name to commemorate Ford's notable victory in the 1970 London to Birmingham Rally. Oh, all right, London to Mexico Rally. What kudos for Dad

YEARS MADE 1967–75 (Mk 1, shown), 1975–80 (Mk 2)

TOP SPEED* 115mph (Escort Mk 1 Twin Cam)

0–60MPH ACCELERATION* 8.9 sec (Escort Mk 1 RS1600)

MAXIMUM POWER* 120bhp (Escort Mk 1 RS1600)

BEST OVERALL FUEL ECONOMY 29mpg (Mk 1 1100 Super)

ORIGINAL PRICE £666 (1100 Super in 1967)

POP FACT The Mk 1 Escort was developed by Ford in Britain. The Mk 2 was a joint effort with Ford in Germany. It's safe to say the Brits came up with the car's code-name: 'Brenda'.

* A more typical Escort for Dads, but still with a little sparkle, would have been the 1300E offering 93mph, 0–60mph in 13 sec and 72bhp of power.

this was, even if his Escort was just a 1.1-litre. 'Son, see that Finnish rally superstar Hannu Mikkola? He drives a car just like Daddy's.'

The Mk 2 Escort continued in much the same vein, using the same basics as the Mk 1 but with a more modern body, a wider range of trims, engines and shapes, and, of course, yet more rallying success, spawning tantalizing showroom spin-offs. The absolute best of these was the glorious RS2000, which had a unique sloping front end with quad headlamps, four-spoke alloy wheels and, in many cases, fantastic headrests that looked sort of like rectangular tennis rackets. As a kid, the mere sight of one of these excited you enough to make a bit of Cresta come out of your nose. And then curse your Dad for only having a boring old 1300L.

13

MORRIS MARINA

(1971–1980)

In a rare moment of paying attention to what everyone else was doing, British Leyland noticed that the Ford Cortina was rather successful. And it was successful because it was utterly conventional. No new-fangled front-wheel drive and fluid-filled suspension here, unlike most of BL's stuff. So they decided to copy it by making a very uncomplicated saloon to muscle in on Ford's patch. They even poached a Ford designer to make it look unthreatening, just like a Cortina.

In principle it was a cunning plan. Unfortunately, time and money were tight, which is why the brand-new Marina lurched on to the scene in 1971 using essentially the same chassis as the 1948 Morris Minor. It was pretty far from dynamic as a result. In fact, if Dad had ever wanted to know what it was like to drive on a lightly gritted ice rink, buying an early Marina would have given him his answer.

In concept, the Marina was no worse than a Cortina, but somehow, in the real world, it was. When it came to cynically flogging simple engineering by dressing it up in a modern frock, Ford was just more practised. BL should have stuck to their clever engineering and stopped pretending to be dumb because in the end it just made them look stupid.

YEARS MADE 1971–80
TOP SPEED 100mph (1.8TC coupé)
0–60MPH ACCELERATION 12.1 sec (1.8TC coupé)
MAXIMUM POWER 95bhp (1.8TC coupé)
BEST OVERALL FUEL ECONOMY 27mpg (1.3 Super four-door)
ORIGINAL PRICE £994 (1.3 Super four-door in 1971)
POP FACT The original Marina brochure carried the tagline 'Beauty with brains behind it'. Unfortunately, the 'brains' standing behind the cars in the accompanying pastoral photo was a flock of sheep. The brochures were destroyed, and reissued once the offending animals had been airbrushed away.

15

AUSTIN 1100

(1962–1973)

You know how it is with the Mini. Prototype modern small car. Landmark of the twentieth century. Work of genius. Blah blah blah. But it should be said that this, the Mini's quieter, more bookish big brother, was actually more intelligent. The basic layout was the same, but the 1100 also had smooth hydrolastic suspension – introduced and then dropped for the Mini – and where its kid brother's looks came through function, the 1100 had a neat body styled by Italian masters Pininfarina. As a whole it was brilliant, and a huge success as a result. Not just with an Austin badge either, because the 1100 – or bigger-engined 1300 – also came as a Morris, MG, Wolseley, Riley or Vanden Plas, so Dad could buy the car that suited his budget, or lack of.

The 1100 was a bedrock of suburban Britain. It looked pleasant, it was nice to drive, and despite being compact enough to fit in a pre-war garage it had enough space inside to accommodate the whole family. It was an attractive, practical, intelligently engineered small car that the nation loved. Well, they loved it at the time. Now all everyone remembers is its show-off, attention grabbing relative, the Mini. Little brothers, eh?

YEARS MADE 1962–73
TOP SPEED 95mph (1300GT)
0–60MPH ACCELERATION 13.5 sec (1300GT)
MAXIMUM POWER 70bhp (1300GT)
BEST OVERALL FUEL ECONOMY 33mpg (1100 four-door)
ORIGINAL PRICE £695 (1100 Super four-door in 1962)
POP FACT An Austin 1100 Countryman was the car to which manic hotelier Basil Fawlty administers a 'damn good thrashing' in the classic 'Gourmet Night' episode of *Fawlty Towers*, screened in October 1975.

HILLMAN AVENGER

(1970–1976)

In the simpler times of the 1970s there was a demand for simpler cars, largely from the accounts departments in large car-makers who wanted to maximize their profits. Hence this, Hillman's attempt to make white bread.

In line with the profit-boosting philosophy behind it, there was nothing flashy about the technical design, although it did have a moderately advanced rear suspension that shamed the cart springs of the Cortina and Marina. Otherwise, it was just vanilla engineering under a handsome, slightly American-looking body wearing – and the importance of this can't be underemphasized – a really cool badge. *Avenger*. 'Morning, Brian, I've just bought myself an AVENGER.' 'Got to dash, Jean, here comes my husband in his AVENGER.' 'My Dad drives an AVENGER.' It was a name the whole family could enjoy.

And just when you thought things couldn't get any better, Hillman brought out a racy special edition with a matt-black bonnet called the Avenger TIGER. Yes! The regular models were still pretty ordinary workaday saloons and estates. But don't forget, they were also called AVENGER. RAAAAAH!

YEARS MADE 1970–76

TOP SPEED * 91mph (1600 GL)

0–60MPH ACCELERATION * 13.7 sec (1600 GL)

MAXIMUM POWER * 69bhp (1600 GL)

BEST OVERALL FUEL ECONOMY 28mpg (1250 Super)

ORIGINAL PRICE £850 (1250 Super four-door in 1970)

POP FACT To keep costs down, the Avenger's engineers didn't go overboard in making its bodyshell super-rigid. As a result, the secret reason you couldn't specify a sunroof on the two-door model was because cutting a hole in the roof made the whole car as floppy as a sleeping cat.

* The limited-production Avenger Tiger offered 107bhp, 110mph, and 0–60mph in 12 sec, but very few Dads had one.

19

VAUXHALL VIVA

(1963–1979)

The first Viva was a bit of a gamble for Vauxhall, thrusting them back into the small-car market they'd been ignoring for years. But thanks to neat looks and good performance, it was a real success. For the second version, they cribbed the Ford formula of keeping things simple but dressing it in a body that resembled a scaled-down version of a glamorous American car. Job's a good 'un. So much so that when the 1970s rolled around, Vauxhall simply reclothed the same bits, creating the third-generation Viva and a car that, like the Mk 3 Ford Cortina, looked about as '70s as possible without actually sticking sideburns to it.

And, just to get Dad idly wishing he was still a single man, there was a groovy coupé spin-off called the Firenza, which later became 5000 per cent cooler when it was given a mean-looking glassfibre droop snoot and a snorty 2.3-litre engine. In truth, this hairy-chested grunter was a bit of an irrelevance, and one that cost Vauxhall dear since the fuel crisis royally skewered sales. But that was hardly the point. The Viva just seemed better when it had a flagship that appeared to be powered not with petrol, but by the great smell of Brut.

YEARS MADE 1963–66 (HA), 1966–70 (HB), 1970–79 (HC, shown)
TOP SPEED 100mph (HB GT)
0–60MPH ACCELERATION 10.7 sec (HB GT)
MAXIMUM POWER 104bhp (HB GT)
BEST OVERALL FUEL ECONOMY 31mpg (HA)
ORIGINAL PRICE £566 (HA deluxe in 1963)
POP FACT The Viva had a spin-off van version, badged as a Bedford, which was so popular – especially with Post Office Telephones, the forerunner of BT – that it easily outlived the regular car, soldiering on until 1983.

AUSTIN ALLEGRO

(1973–1983)

The Austin 1100 looked pretty, drove well and was massively popular. Then British Leyland replaced it with the Allegro, which was none of those things. What you're looking at here is the car equivalent of running the whole length of the football pitch and walloping one straight into the back of your own net.

The 1970s wasn't a halcyon time for dynamic family cars, but Alfa-Romeo's Alfasud had already shown that a compact front-wheel-drive car could be a pleasure rather than a chore, and just a year after the Allegro the VW Golf pulled off the same trick, which showed up BL's bulbous sloth as the missed opportunity it was.

Dad did, however, have one stout reason for buying it over the Alfa or VW: it was British. So our plucky lads at BL spent half their time outside the factory chanting union slogans about fair pay and softer loo rolls, but when father finally got his Allegro at least he knew he hadn't defected to Johnny bloody Foreigner with his dastardly habit of making a nice-looking car that people actually wanted. BL used to do that too, of course. But then they replaced it with this. Dah!

YEARS MADE 1973–83

TOP SPEED 100mph (1750)

0–60MPH ACCELERATION 11.4 sec (1750)

MAXIMUM POWER 90bhp (1750)

BEST OVERALL FUEL ECONOMY 31mpg (1100)

ORIGINAL PRICE £974 (1100 two-door in 1973)

POP FACT One of the great 'facts' about the Allegro is that it's supposedly more aerodynamic in reverse than going forwards. Which it probably is, but then so would many cars with a snub nose and rounded tail.

23

HILLMAN HUNTER
(1966–1976)

Hillman's owners, the Rootes Group, had a history of gaffes, most famously, in the aftermath of the Second World War when the British army offered company boss, Lord Rootes, the chance to assess a car they'd discovered in a captured German factory. Rootes declared that it was an unattractive design and would not have a fruitful life. That car was the VW Beetle, and after 21 million cars over 58 years of continuous production, you'd have to say he was wrong.

More pertinently, the company made another error in the early '60s when they rushed the radical Hillman Imp into production and paid the price for its shabby reliability. That had a direct effect on the Hunter, which had to be kept simple and reliable. Hence an utterly rational car for the utterly rational Dad. Just one who didn't fancy a Cortina. But that was fine, because the Hunter was a stout servant, more so than its creators ever envisaged. It may have disappeared from Britain in the mid-'70s, but the Hunter enjoyed a second life in Iran where – called the Paykan – it soldiered on until 2005, having been pretty much the sole transport of an entire nation for almost 40 years. And even the Ford Cortina would be hard-pressed to claim that.

YEARS MADE 1966–76

TOP SPEED 105mph (Hunter GLS)

0–60MPH ACCELERATION 10.5 sec (Hunter GLS)

MAXIMUM POWER 95bhp (Hunter GLS)

BEST OVERALL FUEL ECONOMY 26.5mpg

ORIGINAL PRICE £838 (in 1966)

POP FACT A Hillman Hunter won the 11,500-mile 1968 London–Sydney Marathon: only 55 of the 98 entries made it all the way, and the Hunter won after the leading car, a Citroën DS, suffered a head-on crash with a Mini.

25

2 SENSIBLE DAD

Dad at his slacks-'n'-slippers wearing best.

DATSUN SUNNY

(1973–1982)

Even into the '70s Japanese cars were viewed with disdain in the UK. They were funny-looking, they were tinny and, most importantly, they just weren't British. Sales were relatively low. But they were on the increase because a growing band of people had spotted the cars' distinct merits, not least that they were as reliable as a Swiss labrador. The Datsun Sunny was the perfect example of this. Yes, it looked strange, especially with those weird, crinkly wheel trims, but Dad had heard good things about its precision engineering, as well as being tempted by its generous equipment levels. This car had – crikey! – a radio as standard, and there weren't many European rivals that could boast such lavish medium-wave modernity.

Unfortunately, as his Datsun dissolved before his very eyes Dad would later discover that the Japanese hadn't got every aspect of car-making completely licked. But, by golly, they were learning fast. And even when his Sunny's body was riddled with rust, at least Dad could be confident that the radio still worked.

YEARS MADE 1973–7 (Type B210, shown), 1977–82 (Type B310)

TOP SPEED 96mph (Type B310 1.4-litre)

0–60MPH ACCELERATION 17 sec approx (Type B310, 1.4-litre)

MAXIMUM POWER 63bhp (Type B310, 1.4-litre)

BEST OVERALL FUEL ECONOMY 33mpg (Type B210 1.2-litre)

ORIGINAL PRICE £1296 (Type B210 coupé in 1974)

POP FACT The Type B210 120Y Sunny was only on sale for four years, but in that time it proved incredibly successful, selling over 2.36 million examples and becoming one of the first Japanese cars to enjoy global domination.

29

VOLKSWAGEN GOLF

(1974–1983)

The Golf was life or death for Volkswagen. For decades they'd relied on the Beetle as their bread and butter and when, at the start of the '70s, the ugly Bug was on the wane, they needed to think fast to stay alive. Deep within their German base some sturdily engineered stops were pulled out and this is what they came up with: a practical, well-engineered small car, set off by the crisp styling of Italian design guru Giorgetto Giugiaro. VW was back in business.

Not that the fiscal health of a large foreign car-maker really mattered to Dad. In fact, supporting the Germans in the mid-'70s felt mildly treasonous, even when the home teams were too busy striking actually to make stuff. No, he just wanted an unusually sturdy and reliable little car, and the warm feeling of beating the system. Back then the VW was an obscure choice and one that said, 'I could have an Escort, but I'm smarter than that.'

Once the Golf had shown how good looks and sound quality could sell small cars, many rivals tried to copy the formula. But Sensible Dad had gone for original and best. If only he could have afforded the cool GTi.

YEARS MADE 1974–83

TOP SPEED 113mph (GTi 1.8-litre)

0–60MPH ACCELERATION 8.9 sec (GTi 1.8-litre)

MAXIMUM POWER 112bhp (GTi 1.8-litre)

BEST OVERALL FUEL ECONOMY 50mpg (diesel)

ORIGINAL PRICE £1517 (1100L in 1975)

POP FACT Like the Passat and the Scirocco, the Golf was another '70s VW named after a wind. In this case, *Golfstrom*, which is German for Gulf Stream.

3

TOYOTA COROLLA
(1970–1984)

Sometimes your Dad could be sooo dull. 'No, you can't play out late.' 'Yes, you *do* have to clear away your toys before bedtime.' And of course, 'Good news everyone, I've just bought a Toyota Corolla.' Even by the standards of the time, this was not a sexy car. In fact it made the Ford Escort seem as exciting as a gold-plated space ship with the Bay City Rollers inside. But that's because you were young, and had a poster of a Ferrari Boxer on your wall.

For Dad, the Corolla was a deeply satisfying way of being sensible. It was reasonably well priced, it had enough equipment and, because it was a Toyota, it was reliable. In fact, in a big list of things that would never ever break, Dad's Corolla was there, one place above Ben Nevis. Not such great compensation for the kids who longed for something a little less cardigan-ish, but Dad hoped that one day maybe they'd appreciate the more sensible things in life. Including an entirely functional car that simply started, drove, and stopped again every time you asked it to. In that sense it really was nothing more than just a bog-standard car. But from Sensible Dad's perspective, what a car.

YEARS MADE 1970–79 (Mk 2), 1980–84 (Mk 3)
TOP SPEED 98mph (Mk 3 1.5-litre)
0–60MPH ACCELERATION 12.1 sec (Mk 3 1.6-litre)
MAXIMUM POWER 86bhp (Mk 3 1.6-litre)
BEST OVERALL FUEL ECONOMY 32mpg (Mk 2 1-litre)
ORIGINAL PRICE £949 (Mk 2 1.3-litre in 1970)
POP FACT The Corolla was the result of fresh thinking after Toyota's abortive first foray into the US in 1958 with the Crown, a car so unsuited to American highways that under sustained driving it literally broke apart.

33

AUSTIN MAXI
(1969–1981)

In many ways this was the very epitome of a Sensible Dad car. Yes, its appearance was about as sexy as a builder's skip but it was also as practical and accommodating as, well, a builder's skip. Thanks to the genius of the bloke who also designed the Mini, British Leyland had come up with one of the world's first hatchbacks, and behind that big tailgate was an interior that could swallow multiple people, bags, pieces of furniture and anything up to and including an adolescent hippo.

Yes, early '70s kids might have preferred to be seen in a Ford Cortina with its pretend American styling and swishy interior, but could Cortina-driving Dad take five bags of grass clippings, half a ton of old magazines and a broken chest of drawers to the tip in one hit? Not likely. So what if the Austin's engines suffered from a touch of asthma and that getting it into gear might require the use of a large hammer? The Maxi was upright, sensible and slightly eccentric. Rather like your Dad, in fact.

YEARS MADE 1969–81
TOP SPEED 97mph (1750)
0–60MPH ACCELERATION 13.2 sec (1750)
MAXIMUM POWER 91bhp (1750)
BEST OVERALL FUEL ECONOMY 26mpg (1500)
ORIGINAL PRICE £1103 (1500 in 1969)
POP FACT The Maxi was done on a budget and one of the most conspicuous cost savings was using all four doors off the older and rather ungainly Austin 1800.

35

3 EXECUTIVE DAD

He made decisions. Like deciding to get a nicer car.

TRIUMPH 2000

(1963–1977)

Triumph might be best remembered for little roadsters but let's not forget that they knew a thing or two about making a decent saloon car too, hence this, the rather excellent Triumph 2000. This was a quietly confident car that gently spoke volumes about your Dad's standing in the world. It said, 'When I'm in the office I don't have to make my own cups of tea.' The 2000 really came into its own in 1969 when it was given a stylish top 'n' tail makeover that previewed the look of the forthcoming, and insanely cool, Stag sports car, but even before that it was handsome and desirable.

Aside from a brief dalliance with a new-fangled fuel-injected engine that didn't work properly, the 2000 was brilliant. Its only real problem came in 1967 when Triumph's owners, British Leyland, bought Rover whose own 2000 was a straight rival. For once BL realized that having two cars in direct competition with each other was a bit silly and commissioned the Rover SD1 to replace both, marking the end of big saloons made by Triumph. Which was a shame, because actually they were rather good at it.

YEARS MADE 1963–77

TOP SPEED 96mph (Mk 2)

0–60MPH ACCELERATION 14.1 sec (Mk 1)

MAXIMUM POWER 90bhp (Mk 1)

BEST OVERALL FUEL ECONOMY 23.5mpg (Mk 1)

ORIGINAL PRICE £1094 (Mk 1 in 1964)

POP FACT There was a spacious estate version of the 2000 (and later 2500) series cars, but it proved surprisingly unpopular. For every 15 saloons sold, only one person bought an estate. These days posh estates are in huge demand so maybe Triumph were just ahead of their time.

39

FORD GRANADA

(1972–1985)

Put 'em away love, it's the Ford Granada. *The Sweeney* has a lot to answer for where this car is concerned: John Thaw and Dennis Waterman raging around in their Consul GT 3.0-litre version cementing the Granada's image as the kind of car that made executive decisions by smashing through someone's front door and belting them in the face. But your Dad probably didn't do that, any more than he might have had a Player's No. 6 and Scotch on toast for breakfast. His Granada was a bit more civilized with its swoopy period styling, set off particularly well by a nice vinyl roof.

For some reason, all Granadas, whether ordinary saloon, strangely decadent coupé or the massive estate, seem to live in the memory as being brown. Other colours were available of course, but the Granada just suited brown. At least until 1977, when Ford binned the nothing-more-'70s original and replaced it with a square-cut Mk 2 version that somehow lacked the you're-nicked-sunshine sleaze appeal of its forebear. Mind you, if Dad really had shouted 'SHUT IT, YOU SLAG!' it's almost certain he would been asked to leave the bridge club.

YEARS MADE 1972–7 (Mk 1, shown), 1977–85 (Mk 2)

TOP SPEED 117mph (Mk 2 2.8i)

0–60MPH ACCELERATION 8.9 sec (Mk 2 2.8i)

MAXIMUM POWER 160bhp (Mk 2 2.8i)

BEST OVERALL FUEL ECONOMY 27mpg (Mk 2 2.3 diesel)

ORIGINAL PRICE £2031 (Mk 1 3-litre GXL in 1972)

POP FACT Granada TV took legal action against Ford for using the same name on this car, but the case was dropped after its chairman Sidney Bernstein drove a Granada and decided that he approved of it.

ROVER SD1

(1976–1986)

You might be forgiven for thinking that the Rover SD1 was styled by children. After all, who else but kids would have the quizzical brilliance to say, 'Well, why *can't* a normal car look like a Ferrari?' You might be forgiven for thinking that the Rover SD1 was also engineered by children because who else but kids would get bored with the whole thing and wander off before it was finished. That happened a lot in the '70s car industry; the difference here was that the lack of quality control undermined something wonderful. And this wasn't all down to those rakish looks. There was also the bassy 3.5-litre V8 engine, throbbing you along at some pace as Dad clasped the odd-shaped steering wheel with its unusual centre, weirdly reminiscent of a massive Opal Fruit. Later on, Rover introduced lesser engines as well, but you needed the man-size V8 to maximize the enormous envy that Dad's SD1 could inspire in any late '70s playground.

If only Rover had had the money to develop it properly, and keep on developing it into the '80s instead of being forced into a weak-kneed, V8-less bunk-up with Honda, maybe they'd still be around today making fabulous-looking cars like this. Because when Rover were on form, they made it look like child's play.

YEARS MADE 1976–86

TOP SPEED 135mph (Vitesse)

0–60MPH ACCELERATION 9.8 sec (Vitesse)

MAXIMUM POWER 190bhp (Vitesse)

BEST OVERALL FUEL ECONOMY 33mpg (2400SD)

ORIGINAL PRICE £4750 (3500 in 1977)

POP FACT When the Rover SD1 came to an end in Britain, the production line was shipped to India, where it returned to life as the Standard 2000 with an old Standard Vanguard motor. It was a complete disaster and only 100 were made.

43

FORD ZEPHYR/ZODIAC

(1962–1972)

There's an apocryphal car-industry story about Ford that goes something like this. Young bloke goes for a job interview with the company and is taken aback when the boss asks him, 'What do we make here?' 'Well, erm, you make cars,' the chap splutters. 'Wrong,' barks the boss, 'we make money.' And here's another example of how they kept that money rolling in. The Zephyr, and its Zodiac brother, were big, impressive-looking cars that, while not the last word in complexity, kept selling because they always looked right for their times. Usually this involved cribbing things off whatever American cars were cool at that particular moment, so through four generations the Zephyr got chromier, then sprouted fins and finally became massive and boxy with quite extraordinary proportions that meant the boot was stubby and dropped away while the vast bonnet was flat as Holland and had about the same surface area. It wasn't exactly much of a looker, but it seemed rather imposing nonetheless, and made it quite clear that Executive Dad was not the sort of chap who would settle for some piddly Cortina.

YEARS MADE 1962–6 (Mk 3), 1966–72 (Mk 4, shown)
TOP SPEED 102mph (Mk 4 Zodiac)
0–60MPH ACCELERATION 11 sec (Mk 4 Zodiac)
MAXIMUM POWER 136bhp (Mk 4 Zodiac)
BEST OVERALL FUEL ECONOMY 27mpg (Mk 4 Zephyr IV)
ORIGINAL PRICE £929 (Mk 3 Zephyr VI in 1962)
POP FACT Both these types of big, old Ford were used in the making of the BBC police show *Z-Cars*, which first aired in 1962, but the 'Z' stood for neither Zephyr – or Zodiac – it was the radio call-sign used by the Lancashire Constabulary.

45

VAUXHALL VICTOR

(1957–1976)

What a strange name for a car. Presumably Vauxhall meant 'victor', as in someone who wins something, rather than the chap who lived next door but one. You remember him, nice fellow, balding, married to Janet? Yes, the one with the bonky eye. Where were we? Oh, yes, Victor the car. Well, it was sort of big and mildly impressive and at one point held claim to being the first European car with a panoramic windscreen. Such things were quite amazing back then, as was the later third-generation Victor, which was sometimes called the 101 on the grounds that it contained – wait for it – 101 improvements over the old model. Who actually sat down and counted? And did they get to 99 and think, You know, this would be a whole lot more impressive if we could get to 101 … I've got it! Make the front door handles, erm, nicer. That's two more right there.

Ah, innocent times. Incidentally, the Victor's sister models included the Nigel, the Alan and the Jonathan. Oh, all right, they didn't.

YEARS MADE 1957–61 (F-type), 1961–64 (FB), 1964–67 (FC, shown), 1967–72 (FD), 1972–76 (FE)

TOP SPEED 104mph (FE 2300)

0–60MPH ACCELERATION 11.3 sec (FE 2300)

MAXIMUM POWER 124bhp (FE 3300)

BEST OVERALL FUEL ECONOMY 32mpg (FB)

ORIGINAL PRICE £758 (F-type in 1957)

POP FACT The early Victors soon gained a terrible reputation for rust because of several unintentional water traps concealed in the body, including one spot where water leaked in through the wraparound windscreen.

47

ROVER 2000

(1963–1973)

For its entire car-making life, Rover had been a sensible, solid company making sensible, solid cars. And then, almost from nowhere, they did this. The radical 2000. It was as startling as coming home to find your Mum stark naked and rolling in paint on the living-room floor. Mind you, it was the '60s so that wasn't entirely out of the question.

Nonetheless, from a staid company like Rover the 2000 was a revelation. As well as some very advanced engineering, it looked terrific, even with the bizarre option of sticking the spare wheel on the bootlid to allow more space for luggage. The interior was special too, with cool, sculpted chairs instead of a bench seat in the back. Yeah, it was like Dad had bought a sports car. Although the one thing the Rover lacked was real performance; at least until it was fitted with a V8 engine to make the 3500, which went as well as it looked.

But even as the plain 2000, this was a landmark moment in Executive Dad's world. It was a Rover, and that made it respectable enough to avoid dark mutterings in the cul-de-sac; it was also enough of a groover to let him pretend he was Peter Sellers.

YEARS MADE 1963–73
TOP SPEED 108mph
0–60MPH ACCELERATION 11.9 sec
MAXIMUM POWER 110bhp
BEST OVERALL FUEL ECONOMY 31mpg
ORIGINAL PRICE £1264 (1963)
POP FACT The 2000 was actually meant to look even more radical than it did. Early prototypes sported a dramatic shark-like nose but Rover bosses were worried this was too outrageous and had it lopped off.

49

4 COMPACT DAD
Maybe you weren't the only little bundle of joy in his life.

MINI CLUBMAN ESTATE

(1969–1982)

The box-fronted Clubman range was meant to be slightly posher than the normal Mini, and to that end Dad could glance manfully at a brand-new set of instruments that were now – shock! – right behind the steering wheel, instead of in the middle of the dashboard as they were on other Minis. This new interior fanciness also extended to the seats, which were covered in a sticky velour-ish fabric that acted like a magnet for ice cream, snot and dog drool. Earlier Clubman estates also came with really strange strips up the side that were meant to look like wood, but the kind of horrible fake wood that a cheap '70s telly might be made of. Presumably this was some sort of weird tribute to the often wood-trimmed Mini Traveller it replaced. It didn't work, and the car looked better when the strips were eventually binned in favour of groovy stick-on stripes.

For Dad, the Clubman estate had two benefits. Firstly, it was a little car but you could cram an awful lot of kids' stuff, and actual kids, inside it. And, secondly, that longer, squared-off nose gave him more spanner room for when he wanted to spend Sunday mornings under the open bonnet, swearing and taking all the skin off his hands.

YEARS MADE 1969–82
TOP SPEED 82mph (1098cc)
0–60MPH ACCELERATION
17.9 sec (1098cc)
MAXIMUM POWER 45bhp (1098cc)
BEST OVERALL FUEL ECONOMY
37mpg (1098cc)
ORIGINAL PRICE £763
(998cc engine in 1969)
POP FACT In a surprisingly high-tech move, the Clubman was the first car to use a printed circuit board in its instrument pack.

53

VAUXHALL CHEVETTE
(1975–1984)

Most cars of the 1970s had front ends as flat as an oven door, but plucky Vauxhall entertained some different ideas. Over in Europe their colleagues at Opel made a near identical car called the Kadett, which had a dull, bluff nose, whereas the Chevette's schnozz was sleek and swept back, heralding a brave new world where everything would be swish and aerodynamic. Even trousers.

The rest of the Chevette was a bit less futuristic, being pretty low tech in fact, but it had a simple charm. Unless, of course, you were one of the kids in the back, in which case you might rue the 'simple charm' of Vauxhall's decision to cover only the central panels of the seats in some models with a racy check cloth, leaving the outer bits upholstered in a special vinyl that on summer days would become hotter than the sun itself. The point at which you discovered you had grown too big to cower on the central cloth, but not so big that you had dispensed with short trousers, was a landmark moment of flesh-searing vinyl–skin interface in the life of any Chevette owner's offspring. More to the point, it really, really hurt.

YEARS MADE 1975–84
TOP SPEED 90mph
0–60MPH ACCELERATION 14.5 sec
MAXIMUM POWER 59bhp
BEST OVERALL FUEL ECONOMY 35mpg
ORIGINAL PRICE £1650
(Chevette L three-door in 1975)
POP FACT During development of the Austin Metro, British Leyland engineers bought a fleet of rival cars for comparison, including a Chevette. It was by far the most crudely engineered, yet in hard testing it was also the one that went wrong the least.

55

AUSTIN METRO

(1980–1990)

In 1980 the Union Jack-makers of Britain worked flat out, not for the impending huzzah-fest of the royal wedding the following year, but to furnish demand from British Leyland as they announced the Metro in a frenzy of patriotic fervour not seen since 1945. The high spot of all the flag waving was a TV ad that depicted a fleet of Metros assembling on the white cliffs of Dover to repel an incoming invasion of foreign small cars, with the strapline 'A British car to beat the world'.

It was jingoistic enough to make your nose run, and in truth the Metro didn't need such king-and-country emotional blackmail because it was a decent little car, even if early ones had weirdly small wheels that made them look as if they were scuttling round on castors.

Unlike the Allegro, the Marina or most of the missed chances BL put out in the '70s, here was a car that really could take on the foreign competition head-to-head. And that meant Dad was buying it because it was good, not just because it was British. Although obviously that did help, especially for the makers of little flags.

YEARS MADE 1980–90
TOP SPEED* 100mph (Metro Vanden Plas)
0–60MPH ACCELERATION* 12.2 sec (Metro Vanden Plas)
MAXIMUM POWER* 72bhp (Metro Vanden Plas)
BEST OVERALL FUEL ECONOMY 38mpg (1.3HLE)
ORIGINAL PRICE £3095 (1.0 basic in 1981)
POP FACT Train-maker Metro Cammell objected to BL using part of its name on a car, hence early models were actually badged 'MiniMetro' until the problem was resolved.
*This model offered identical performance to the MG Metro, whose engine it shared, but for real speed-freak Dads there was the MG Metro Turbo, offering 110mph top speed and 0–60mph in 10.3 sec from its 93bhp engine.

57

HILLMAN IMP

(1963–1976)

The Imp was Hillman's answer to the Mini, but it was an answer that suggested they might have been paying attention to an entirely different question. Yes, it was small, but rather than copy its rival's clever and compact front-wheel-drive design the Imp was rear-wheel drive and had its engine at the back and a boot at the front. For kids this was notable as a source of amusement – 'Daaad, why are you putting bags under the bonnet?' – or maybe just confusion – 'Daaad, why is the engine in the wrong place?'

The Imp itself was surprisingly racy, what with its race-tuned chassis and all-aluminium motor. It was even quite nippy, if you revved it. However, revving it was also inviting it to break because the Imp was famously temperamental and had a pretty distant relationship with build quality. A brand-new Scottish factory with an inexperienced workforce didn't help on that score, nor did a rush to get it on sale, which meant the whole thing came out rather half baked.

This was a shame because at heart the Imp was a nippy little car, and one that meant when Dad was driving alone he could secretly pretend he was Stirling Moss.

YEARS MADE 1963–76

TOP SPEED 80mph

0–60MPH ACCELERATION 23.7 sec

MAXIMUM POWER 39bhp

BEST OVERALL FUEL ECONOMY 38mpg

ORIGINAL PRICE £508 (in 1963)

POP FACT As well as its 'boot' space under the bonnet, the Imp offered a rear screen that could lift up like a hatchback, through which bags of shopping could be dumped on to its rear seat. Or children's heads.

59

FORD ANGLIA 105E

(1959–1967)

Otherwise known as the 'Harry Potter car', in its day the Anglia was slightly less magical, being an honest and unsophisticated little car for Dads everywhere. There was nothing especially radical about its engineering – next to the Mini, also launched in 1959, it was as dumb as a box of rocks – but it employed Ford's usual cunning trick of bog-standard mechanical parts to keep the price and running costs low, garnished with a smart and moderately desirable body. In this case, the designers went nuts with their copy of the Big Book of American Cars, shamelessly nicking all the flashy bits from 1950s US land yachts and shrinking them to a size that would actually fit into Britain. Hence the leering chrome mouth, smart side stripe, inward slanted back window and cheeky fins on either side of the bootlid.

It looks antique today, but there was a time when these things would warm the cockles of a stylish Dad's heart. The Anglia was fundamentally an uncomplicated car, but it looked good, it didn't cost the earth and it got the job done. Oh, yeah, and despite what the movies might lead you to believe, it couldn't fly. Not unless your Muggle Dad had somehow fathered a wizard.

YEARS MADE 1959–67

TOP SPEED 83mph (Anglia Super)

0–60MPH ACCELERATION 20.8 sec (Anglia Super)

MAXIMUM POWER 48.5bhp (Anglia Super)

BEST OVERALL FUEL ECONOMY 36mpg (Anglia standard)

ORIGINAL PRICE £610 (Anglia standard in 1959)

POP FACT Apart from its role in the Harry Potter phenomenon, the 105E Anglia's other contribution to popular culture was in the 1982 BBC2 sit-com *The Young Ones*, where a customized version was driven by insane punk Vyvyan, played by Adrian Edmondson.

5 LUXURY DAD
My Dad's richer than your Dad, so nurrr.

BMW 5-SERIES
(1972–1981)

There was something quite brave about buying a German car in the mid-'70s. Not specifically because it was German – the war had been over for 30 years – but because it just seemed a bit, well, unpatriotic. But it was cars like this that started Britain's love affair with stout Germanic saloons and the 5-series very neatly defined what people like about them. It didn't look especially adventurous, in fact it was a bit dour and upright, but it had a certain aggression, like a shark in a carp pond. The inside was even more strait-laced, being as colourful and welcoming as the inside of a Victorian chimney, although it also felt as solid as a Victorian chimney. For Dad, however, the real draw was the hearty six-cylinder engine and the sense that the whole car had been designed by people who wanted driving to be fun.

The 5-series was actually a bit sporty, but if Dad carefully ordered the car in a discreet colour your mother need never know that. He'd also have to hide the dealer's invoice, otherwise she might notice that BMW managed to charge more for a car that had less kit than most rivals. But then that's a trick the Germans have been pulling off for years, even if their cars don't look like sharks any more.

YEARS MADE 1972–81
TOP SPEED 124mph (528)
0–60MPH ACCELERATION 9 sec (528)
MAXIMUM POWER 170bhp (528)
BEST OVERALL FUEL ECONOMY 21mpg (518)
ORIGINAL PRICE £3299 (520 in 1974)
POP FACT The distinctive bend in the back edge of a BMW's side-window is known as the 'Hofmeister kink', named after former BMW design boss Wilhelm Hofmeister who introduced it to the company's cars in 1961.

65

MERCEDES-BENZ 200

(1975–1982)

In an era when the quality of cars could be as variable as British weather, one model stood apart, strong and mighty like an oak in a field of pampas grass. It was the Mercedes 200, less a car and more a kind of noble edifice with wheels. The 200 didn't feel like it was assembled. It felt like Mercedes had taken delivery of a massive solid-metal billet and then slowly carved it into the shape of a rather boxy car. This was the family bus that the kids couldn't destroy. Sure, over time the seats might get a bit worn-in and springy but still the mighty Merc forged on, starting and stopping as precisely as the day it was made. Kids boinged around on the bench in the back, often fetchingly trimmed in check cloth, while Dad sat up front, hands lightly gripping the massive wheel, using the three-pointed star at the end of the bonnet as a rifle sight, focused on weaker cars in his way.

The Merc wasn't actually that luxurious, but it had more than mere trimmings. It had a feeling of safety and sanctuary that would last for ever. As the simmering threat of nuclear war grew during the '70s and early '80s you could easily believe that when the bombs dropped the only things to survive would be cockroaches and your Dad's Mercedes 200.

YEARS MADE 1975–82
TOP SPEED 100mph
0–60MPH ACCELERATION 15 sec
MAXIMUM POWER 94bhp
BEST OVERALL FUEL ECONOMY 20mpg
ORIGINAL PRICE £4940 (in 1976)
POP FACT In 1976 this was one of the most expensive 2-litre saloons you could buy, costing £2000 more than the £2928 Ford Granada 2000L. And it still didn't have a radio as standard.

67

JAGUAR XJ6

(1968–1986)

Now here was your real Luxury Dad moment. Those German luxo-cars, they weren't all that lavish inside; in truth, unless Dad splashed his cash on optional extras they could be as cosy as the lifts in a council tower-block. The 'luxury' bits were really the price and the cut-above badge on the front. Whereas with Jaguar, you got the real deal. The woodwork, the leather, the overwhelming sense of being purred around in the Bodleian Library. It was splendid. And exciting too, what with that bank of mysterious switches on the dash, one of which toggled between two separate fuel tanks. It needed them too, because the Jag liked its juice even more than Dad liked a G&T of an evening. Still, at least there was a pay-off because where lesser cars spluttered and yelped, the Jag emitted a soothing hum as Dad gently summoned up his well-heeled six-cylinder power.

The XJ6's heyday was the '70s, at least until Jaguar was sucked into the horror of British Leyland, at which point what little car-building actually happened was to a distinctly casual standard. But kids didn't care about that. They could just enjoy the silence, the leather seats, and the knowledge that Dad knew true luxury when he saw it.

YEARS MADE 1968–86

TOP SPEED 131mph (Series 3 4.2-litre)

0–60MPH ACCELERATION 8.6 sec (Series 3 4.2-litre)

MAXIMUM POWER 205bhp (Series 3 4.2-litre)

BEST OVERALL FUEL ECONOMY 17mpg (Series 1 2.8-litre)

ORIGINAL PRICE £2400 (Series 1 3.4-litre in 1969)

POP FACT Jaguar's engineers made opening the bonnet on a Sunday morning a moment of pride – the camshaft covers and inlet manifold were polished alloy, and the exhaust manifolds were black enamelled.

RANGE ROVER

(1970–1996)

In some circles this car wouldn't be celebrated at all. Given that it pretty much invented the idea of a more refined and fashionable 4×4, in some British towns people might want to put it in the stocks so it could be pelted with rocks and hot Ribena. Which is unfair on the original Range Rover because it wasn't meant to be a fashion statement, and wasn't all that luxurious either. Compared to the Land-Rover, whose interior was as comfy as sleeping in a river, the Range Rover did have a smidge more refinement to it, but it was still designed to be cleaned out with a mop and bucket. Trouble was, people still thought it was rather cool and Land-Rover spent the rest of the '70s making it more and more townie friendly until, by the early 1980s, it had become a lavish, five-door luxo machine like no other.

Even early models gave Dad the innate sense of superiority that comes from looking down on others, as well as the innate sense of impending bankruptcy every time he went to feed yet more fuel to that fabulous but rather gluttonous V8 engine. The Range Rover became a status symbol, and increasingly a figure of hate, way beyond what its inventors had ever imagined. But don't blame the car for that.

YEARS MADE 1970–96
TOP SPEED 110mph (4.2-litre)
0–60MPH ACCELERATION 10.8 sec (4.2-litre)
MAXIMUM POWER 200bhp (4.2-litre)
BEST OVERALL FUEL ECONOMY 21mpg (2.5-litre Turbo D)
ORIGINAL PRICE £1998 (3.5-litre in 1970)
POP FACT The original Range Rover was seen as such a superb piece of industrial design that one was exhibited in the Louvre as an example of modern sculpture.

TRIUMPH DOLOMITE

(1972–1980)

The Germans might think they own the idea of a sporty but luxurious small saloon but they're wrong because here we have one of the first examples of the idea that bred the BMW 3-Series and Audi A4. And it isn't German at all, although the formula was the same, as follows:

Start with smart looks, which the Dolomite certainly had, in a modest sort of way. Give it a well-turned interior with dashes of raciness, such as the Dolomite's saucy three-spoke wheel and the bank of instruments across its wooden dash. Finally, make sure it has good handling and a turn of speed. No faulting the Dolomite there either, especially when they introduced the remarkable Sprint version, the first mainstream car to have four valves per cylinder and also the first British saloon to have alloy wheels, as standard. Stop laughing, that was once genuinely exciting.

Perhaps mindful of this, Triumph later calmed things down with less racy 1300 and 1500 models to balance out the 1850 and Sprint. And, like all Dolomites, they were attractive cars built to an interesting formula. Probably particularly interesting if you were watching from, say, BMW or Audi.

YEARS MADE 1972–80
TOP SPEED 115mph (Dolomite Sprint)
0–60MPH ACCELERATION 8.7 sec (Dolomite Sprint)
MAXIMUM POWER 127bhp (Dolomite Sprint)
BEST OVERALL FUEL ECONOMY 31.1mpg (Dolomite 1300)
ORIGINAL PRICE £1399 (1850 in 1972)
POP FACT In early episodes of *The Professionals*, Bodie drove a Dolomite. However, when the show's producers got sick of British Leyland sending over a different-coloured car for each block of filming they called Ford, who actually understood the idea of continuity, and gave them the same Capri for as long as they wanted.

73

6 **DEMOB** DAD

Dad cars got groovy as rationing came to an end.

AUSTIN CAMBRIDGE

(1959–1969)

The original Austin Cambridge, and its Morris Oxford equivalent, was a perfectly ordinary car that fitted neatly into the steady recovery of war-torn mid-'50s Britain. It was functional at a time when people had more exciting things to think about, like the prospect of eating bananas again. It wasn't until the end of the '50s that the Cambridge got a lot more interesting thanks, bizarrely, to the Duke of Edinburgh.

It was Her Majesty's Him Indoors who, on an official visit to Austin in 1955, pointedly told boss Sir Leonard Lord that the secret car designs he'd just been shown weren't as attractive as the foreign competition. Lord was so stung by the regal critique that the next day he called master Italian designers Farina and asked them to help. And that's how the Cambridge went from an unremarkable wallflower to the striking, fin-wearing re-body of 1959.

It was still a simple, unremarkable car underneath but the stylish new shell made it vastly more appealing. It wasn't quite the equivalent of Captain Mainwaring turning into Sophia Loren, but at the very least the Cambridge had become an urbane Sergeant Wilson.

YEARS MADE 1959–61 (A55/Morris Oxford V, shown), 1961–9 (A60/Morris Oxford VI)
TOP SPEED 81mph (A60)
0–60MPH ACCELERATION 21.4 sec (A60)
MAXIMUM POWER 61bhp (A60)
BEST OVERALL FUEL ECONOMY 37mpg (Morris Oxford diesel)
ORIGINAL PRICE £830 (A55 in 1959)
POP FACT When the A55 was replaced by the almost identical A60 model, there was one subtle style change: the rear wings were cunningly slimmed down to lose those by-then unfashionable tailfins. The Cambridge–Oxford was, at the time, the only British car available with a diesel engine.

STANDARD

STANDARD VANGUARD

(1955–1963)

The Standard Vanguard of the 1940s and beyond proved one very clear truth that existed in British car-building for many decades. If you want to make a pretty basic and rather dull model seem suddenly glamorous and exciting, and not as dispiriting as February in Morecambe, make it look American. Hell, yeah. Designing a car that resembled a sort of boil-washed refugee from Detroit was instant excitement made metal, and until the 1970s everyone was at it.

But the Vanguard had more of an excuse than many, coming so soon after the Second World War when memories of all those GIs domiciled in Britain was still fresh in the mind. They had seemed somehow exotic and interesting, and the Vanguard could ride that wave of Yank-based enthusiasm. It was technically quite modern for its time too, even if its compact size and four-cylinder engine made it pretty far from the massive V8-powered monsters actual Americans drove. But British drivers weren't too fussed about that. They'd got a car with a subtle flavour of the United States that could have been enhanced only if it had started trying to flog them chewing gum and nylons.

YEARS MADE 1955–8 (Vanguard III), 1958–63 (Vanguard Vignale/Six)

TOP SPEED 90mph (Vanguard Six)

0–60MPH ACCELERATION 19.7 sec (Vanguard Six)

MAXIMUM POWER 80bhp (Vanguard Six)

BEST OVERALL FUEL ECONOMY 30mpg (Vanguard III)

ORIGINAL PRICE £938 (Vanguard III in 1955)

POP FACT This Vanguard was one of the first British cars to be bought for fleet use, especially by the RAF, which snapped up large numbers of them for its staff.

79

VAUXHALL CRESTA/VELOX

(1957–1972)

Cresta the drink was, at least according to the inexplicable polar bear that advertised it, 'Frothy, man!' Cresta the car, erm, wasn't. In fact, it was just a poshed-up version of the cheaper Velox model and boasted such excitements as, oooh, a clock. Be still my fast-beating mid-'50s heart. Happily, in 1957 things got a lot frothier with the introduction of a revised Cresta, called the PA, which was a riot of fins, wrap-around windscreens, white-wall tyres and all the things that made American cars seem so outrageous – but on something you could actually buy here in the good ol' UK of A. Well, a wop-bop-a-loo-bop-a-wop-bam-boo! If you wanted a design that captured the very essence of the late '50s, this was it. It was a long Edwardian jacket, drainpipe jeans and thick crêpe-soled shoes in car form.

In fact, Vauxhall attempted to go even further by fitting later model Crestas with a massive DA hairstyle on top, but Brylcreem were unable to provide a fixative that could prevent unwanted quiff movement at speeds of up to 70mph. Oh, all right, that's a lie. Actually Vauxhall replaced the PA Cresta with a new model called the PB in 1962 and for some reason it just wasn't half as exciting. Shame.

YEARS MADE 1957–62 (PA), 1962–5 (PB), 1965–72 (PC, shown)

TOP SPEED 103mph (PC Cresta)

0–60MPH ACCELERATION 11.6 sec (PB Cresta 3.3–litre)

MAXIMUM POWER 125bhp (PC Cresta)

BEST OVERALL FUEL ECONOMY 22.3mpg (PA Cresta)

ORIGINAL PRICE £984 (PA Velox in 1957)

POP FACT American car-style features that came with the PA Cresta included a steering-column-mounted gearlever, a front bench seat, two-tone paint and upholstery in something called Elastofab. Which was basically nylon.

83

FORD POPULAR/PREFECT

(1953–1961)

In the general evolution of the car the Ford Popular was some kind of tiny dinosaur. Uncomplicated to the point of crudeness and bound for extinction. But it was perfect for the times, when cars were hard to come by and having a vehicle of any kind was seen as pretty swish. Even one as basic as this. The Pop did without fancy trimmings, up to and including a heater, but it was transport, and that was all people really needed.

The technology was distinctly pre-war, including an ancient side-valve engine that was hardly over-burdened with power. But unlike the Ford Popular it replaced, at least it did away with a separate chassis to make the ride that little less bone-shaking. The Prefect, its four-door brother, had already been around for five years, and the two cars shared almost identically plain looks; a bit less vintage character to remind Dad about the good old days of empty roads and powdered egg, but at least the hydraulic brakes could pull the Prefect and Popular to a halt without fear of an instant family wipe-out. Still, at least he was sheltered from the rain in there. And that was one of the best things about the Popular. It wasn't fancy or sophisticated, but at least it kept you relatively dry.

YEARS MADE 1953–59 (Prefect 100E), 1959–61 (Popular 100E)
TOP SPEED 70mph (Popular)
0–60MPH ACCELERATION 30 sec (Popular)
MAXIMUM POWER 36bhp
BEST OVERALL FUEL ECONOMY 33.8mpg (Prefect)
ORIGINAL PRICE £560 (Prefect in 1955)
POP FACT These little Fords were the last to feature side-valve engines, an ancient piece of engineering that went well with the pre-historic three-speed gearbox.

83

ROVER P4
(1949–1964)

If there are two words that can sum up this Rover they would have to be 'bank' and 'manager'. But that's not a criticism; indeed it's more of an endorsement of the car's solid, sensible and thoroughly respectable image. The P4 – actually badged throughout its life as Rover 60, 75, 80, 90, 95, 100, 105 and 110 depending on the engine – was the epitome of stout middle-class values in post-war Britain. Handsome, but not flashy. Slightly luxurious inside, but nothing too decadent. Very early cars did have a moment of wackiness with a strange third headlight in the middle of the grille, but they soon got rid of that Cyclopean mucking about, thank you very much. Otherwise, the P4 was a completely sensible and sternly reassuring presence outside any household. Sort of starchy, but not completely without charm.

Funnily enough, in the 1990s Rover tried to invoke some of those solid P4-ish middle-England values by launching a new car called, like some P4s, the 75. Unfortunately, it wasn't quite successful enough to prevent the company from eventually going belly up. Which is strange, because respectable bank managers still need cars.

YEARS MADE 1949–64
TOP SPEED 100mph (110)
0–60MPH ACCELERATION 15.9 sec (110)
MAXIMUM POWER 123bhp (110)
BEST OVERALL FUEL ECONOMY 27mpg (80)
ORIGINAL PRICE £1106 (75 in 1951)
POP FACT Most P4s had aluminium rather than steel body panels because Rover designed this car, and the Land-Rover, in the 1940s and wanted to take advantage of stocks of surplus aluminium from wartime aircraft production.

85

7 '80s DAD

For the decade as futuristic as Phil Oakey's haircut.

FORD SIERRA

(1982–1993)

If comic books were to be believed the 1980s was the decade in which we'd all be living on the moon, eating food in pill form. Or, if you believed George Orwell, the decade in which you'd end up with a face full of rats. Either way, it was going to be an interesting time and Ford needed to replace the Cortina with something to match. Enter the Sierra and its frankly astonishing styling. Too astonishing for some as it turned out, and the inspiration behind its cheeky nickname, 'the jelly mould'.

Like the more conventional Cortina before it, the Sierra came in a vast range of models, which meant Dad could accurately telegraph his financial status, or at least his standing in the company-car hierarchy between miserable base-spec and lounge-lizard Ghia version. Or, if he were really splashing the cash, he might have gone for the three-door XR4i: 2.8 litres of rippling V6 dressed up with alloy wheels, two-tone paint and a weird but strangely cool two-tier rear spoiler. The designer of this car later admitted that he'd been inspired by the Porsche 928 coupé, which does seem to be pushing it a bit. The Sierra was rakish, but it wasn't *that* rakish.

YEARS MADE 1982–93

TOP SPEED* 127mph (XR4×4)

0–60MPH ACCELERATION*
8.2 sec (XR4×4)

MAXIMUM POWER* 150bhp (XR4×4)

BEST OVERALL FUEL ECONOMY
51mpg (1.6 E)

ORIGINAL PRICE £4783 (1300 in 1982)

POP FACT The man who led the Sierra styling team is now chief designer at Renault, while the bloke who sketched the XR4i model went on to be responsible for the look of all current Volvos.

* The Sierra Cosworth RS500 offered 149mph, 0–60mph in 6.0 sec, and 224bhp, but most Dads had committed the extra money it cost to a kitchen extension.

89

AUSTIN MONTEGO

(1984–1987)

This was Austin-Rover's weapon in the battle against the Sierra and Cavalier for '80s Dad-car supremacy. Unfortunately, the Montego's gestation didn't go well, not when its designer was fired and his replacement insisted that nothing less than a complete redesign was needed to make it successful. He was promptly told to stop causing trouble, and what little changes he could effect before it went on sale didn't do much to make this car a looker, even compared to the outlandish Sierra.

Shame really because under the gawky body the Montego was a decent car. The interior was quite plush, there was loads of room in the back and the top models came with none-more-'80s digital instruments, which were as exciting as getting a ZX Spectrum for Christmas.

Nonetheless, the Montego always felt like the ugly sister in the Sierra/Cavalier/Montego triumvirate and no amount of fiddling – snorty MG turbo, Rover-esque two-tone paint, advertising it with a bloke doing handbrake turns round the office car park – could really sex it up. Maybe they should have let the new bloke redesign when he asked to.

YEARS MADE 1984–7

TOP SPEED 115mph (Vanden Plas EFi)

0–60MPH ACCELERATION 9.1 sec (Vanden Plas EFi)

MAXIMUM POWER 115bhp (Vanden Plas EFi)

BEST OVERALL FUEL ECONOMY 26mpg (1.3L)

ORIGINAL PRICE £5660 (1.6L in 1984)

POP FACT The Montego estate had the option of two rear-facing kids' seats in the boot, just like those posho Mercs that cost twice as much.

RENAULT 18

(1978–1986)

Even at the dawn of the '80s buying anything other than a British car was seen as a bit left field, like ordering moules marinière when there was perfectly good pie and chips on the menu. For Dad to buy French marked him out as something of a freethinker. Maybe he also hankered after a packet of Gauloises and a mucky weekend with Brigitte Bardot, but since your mum would never allow either he'd have to settle for a Renault 18. And what he was actually getting here was the mystique of a foreign badge, stuck to a pretty dull car. But that was deliberate because Renault wanted to sell it in as many countries as they could, and that would never happen if it were infused with other-side-of-the-Channel eccentricity. Nope, mainstream and populist was the order of the day here, like a French chef who'd discovered he could sell a lot more steak tartare if he cooked it and made it into burgers.

Mind you, there were still little touches such as shunning meat-'n'-veg model names like L and GL in favour of the more exotic TL and TS. But apart from that these were pretty ordinary saloons and estates. With just a hint of garlic.

YEARS MADE 1978–86

TOP SPEED 121mph (turbo)

0–60MPH ACCELERATION 10.1 sec (turbo)

MAXIMUM POWER 125bhp (turbo)

BEST OVERALL FUEL ECONOMY 36mpg (2.1-litre turbodiesel)

ORIGINAL PRICE £3313 (1.4TL in 1979)

POP FACT Although the last European Renault 18 was made in 1989, the car soldiered on for another five years over in Argentina.

93

FORD ESCORT MK 3

(1980–1990)

1980 was an exciting year. J. R. got shot, Sinclair invented the home computer, and two definitively '80s cars were born. The Austin Metro was one; this was the other. Goodbye dull and slightly brown '70s, welcome to the clean, crisp '80s.

The Mk 3 Escort summed up a lot of what was expected of the coming decade. Everything was going to be high tech and by 1987 we'd all be sharing our homes with robots or something, so Ford made the Escort high tech too, with front-wheel drive and independent suspension. Actually other car-makers had been doing this stuff for years, but Ford was never a company to rush things.

The real cleverness was the creation of the sporty XR3 model, which, with its black rear spoiler and alloy wheels like a mirror image of Mickey Mouse's ears, became the coolest car of, oooh, October 1980. Like other Escorts, it wasn't perfect to start with but they fixed the problems, introduced an Essex-tastic cabriolet, and then phased in grown-up options like anti-lock brakes and a heated windscreen. Ooh, the superficial sheen of style and high tech. In other words, perfect for the 1980s.

YEARS MADE 1980–90
TOP SPEED 122mph (RS Turbo)
0–60MPH ACCELERATION 8.1 sec (RS turbo)
MAXIMUM POWER 132bhp (RS turbo)
BEST OVERALL FUEL ECONOMY 50mpg (1.6-litre diesel)
ORIGINAL PRICE £4021 (1300L in 1980)
POP FACT For a workaday car, the Mk 3 Escort had some surprisingly famous owners including XR3-loving former Chancellor Kenneth Clarke and princess-to-be Lady Diana Spencer, who was given a top-of-the-range Ghia model as an engagement present by Prince Charles.

95

CAVALIER GLS

VAUXHALL CAVALIER MK 2

(1981–1988)

The first Vauxhall Cavalier forever lived in the shadow of its bitter rival, the Ford Cortina. But with the second-generation model, Vauxhall hit the jackpot because people really seemed to like it. Just as importantly, they *didn't* like Ford's Cortina replacement, the Sierra. Suddenly Dads were flocking to Vauxhall for a stout, normal-looking family car. No Ford aero nonsense here, thanks.

In basic form, the Cav was pretty bleak, its dashboard covered in lots of blanks that left you dreaming of what exciting buttons might be there in more expensive versions. But posher models were more lavish, more veloury and more useful for telling the neighbours things were going pretty well, thanks for asking. British playgrounds might even have rung with taunts like, 'Has your Dad's car got a tilt *and* slide sunroof? Mine has.'

Yet, like many dedicated workhorses, the Cavalier Mk 2 fell from grace pretty fast. Over 800,000 were sold yet by 2006 a survey showed most had long gone, making it one of the most scrapped cars in Britain. And we still hadn't found out what all those blanked-off switches were for.

YEARS MADE 1981–8

TOP SPEED 120mph (SRi 130)

0–60MPH ACCELERATION
8.7 sec (SRi 130)

MAXIMUM POWER 130bhp (SRi 130)

BEST OVERALL FUEL ECONOMY
46mpg (1.6-litre diesel)

ORIGINAL PRICE £4165
(1300L four-door in 1981)

POP FACT Around the world the Mk 2 Cavalier could be had, lightly modified, as a Cadillac, a Chevrolet, a Holden, an Isuzu, an Oldsmobile and an Opel.

97

FRUGAL DAD

Tighter than the knots he tied in your shoelaces.

CITROËN 2CV

(1949–1990)

The Tin Snail was a much maligned car, especially in its twilight years of the 1980s. Somehow it got tarred with a funny Ban-the-Bomb image, but that didn't stop it being a fantastic Frugal Dad's car. It was cheap, it was easy to fix and it made a noise like a dozen playing cards stuck in the wheels of a bicycle. If he drove a 2CV, Dad's wallet saw light of day so rarely it could become home to a colony of moles.

As the 2CV loped along on its bungy suspension, kids slid around on the thin seats that could also be removed from the car and used for an impromptu picnic or something. Although if Dad did that what would you stand on when you posed for photos, proudly poking your head out of the roll-back sunroof?

More lavish Dads would have to spend a fortune on a soft-top car, yet here was your family bouncing along on a budget with the sun gently balming their faces. Who'd have thought frugality could be fun? But the 2CV was more than fun. It was a metal pet with cute bug-eyes. If Dad bought one your family had a new member, probably called something like Minty or Jacques. It was just that sort of car.

YEARS MADE 1949–90
TOP SPEED 68mph (2CV6)
0–60MPH ACCELERATION 31.7 sec (2CV6)
MAXIMUM POWER 29bhp (2CV6)
BEST OVERALL FUEL ECONOMY 37.8mpg (2CV6)
ORIGINAL PRICE £565 (2CV in 1954), £830 (2CV6 in 1974)
POP FACT A yellow 2CV was the star of a chase sequence in the Bond movie *For Your Eyes Only*. The stunt cars needed more power so were fitted with the larger four-cylinder engine from the Citroën GS.

LADA

(1970-1984)

When it came to Britain in 1974 there was a certain novelty value to this chunky Russian. Buying one was even a little brave. A Communist car from behind the Iron Curtain? Why don't you just bloody move to Murmansk, comrade? But in its favour, the Lada was cheap and it appeared to be rugged, built to survive 50 winters on the great steppe. Actually, while the basics might have been sturdy, the Lada wasn't that dependable thanks to Russian build quality as approximate as trying to predict the weather for 2 July 2045. Not that the Soviets hadn't tried. The Lada was based on the Fiat 124 of the mid-'60s, but to prepare it for life under the hammer and sickle they'd beefed up its chassis and engine, in the process smothering whatever Italian finesse it might have had in the first place.

Nonetheless, by the early '80s Ladas became more and more popular. But that didn't make them good, only a good subject for a joke. Despite this, or perhaps bloody-mindedly because of it, Lada owners really seemed to love their cars. For the kids in the back it was a different story. Like the horrendous shorts your Dad insisted on wearing when it was hot, this car was just a bit embarrassing.

YEARS MADE 1970–84
TOP SPEED 97mph (1600)
0-60MPH ACCELERATION 14.0 sec (1600)
MAXIMUM POWER 78bhp (1600)
BEST OVERALL FUEL ECONOMY 26mpg (1200)
ORIGINAL PRICE £981 (1200 in 1975)
POP FACT Lada stopped selling cars in Britain in 1997 when their engines failed to meet new emissions laws, but this ancient car is still in production in Togliatti, Russia, to this very day.

103

RELIANT ROBIN

(1974–1982)

If you really wanted your child to be picked on at school you could try naming them Poo or waiting until they were asleep and dying their hair blue. Or you could drive them around in a three-wheeled car. Yep, that should do it. The bizarre thing about the Robin was that, despite having only three-quarters the number of wheels of a normal car, it wasn't three-quarters the price. Certainly, for the cost of a new one you could have had a pretty recent second-hand car with a wheel at each corner. So buying a Robin was a very deliberate choice, even though the running costs were lower than a snake's belly. There were other things in its favour too. The body was glassfibre so it would never rust and, erm … No, that's it. Otherwise the Robin was a car only for misers who were so terrified of metal rot and petrol stations that to avoid either they'd risk looking very silly.

The three-wheel layout didn't just give this Reliant the sharp cornering ability of a first-time ice-skater either; it also made it useless for negotiating rural tracks with a ridge of grass running up the centre. As a result the Robin was almost certainly not popular with farmers. Or indeed anyone. Apart from cruel parents.

YEARS MADE 1974–82

TOP SPEED 72mph (850)

0–60MPH ACCELERATION 17.3 sec (850)

MAXIMUM POWER 40bhp (850)

BEST OVERALL FUEL ECONOMY 55mpg (850)

ORIGINAL PRICE £801 (750 in 1976)

POP FACT Reliant also made a four-wheeled version of the Robin called the Kitten. Aside from the benefits of 25 per cent more wheel, it actually looked quite groovy, yet it never caught on and lived for just seven years, whereas the Robin and its three-wheeled successors soldiered on for almost another 30.

105

RENAULT 4

(1961–1993)

The Renault 4 might almost have been considered the more luxurious Dad's Citroën 2CV. Although, since the 2CV itself was as luxurious as a North Korean prison, that wasn't saying much. But what the 4 lacked in outright creature comforts, it made up for in other very unusual and very French ways. The gear lever, for example, poked from the dashboard in a 2CV-ish way that was unfathomable to a young mind. The windows slid backwards on runners instead of winding down as they had on most cars since the 1930s. The way the bonnet tipped forwards seemed slightly odd and different too.

But these little quirks just made the 4 lovable as it lolloped along on its soft springs, engine clattering away up front, Dad manfully manipulating that extraordinary gear handle while everyone in the back perched on seats upholstered in slippery vinyl or, on some models, a slightly racy tartan pattern. Yes, the massive panel gaps rendered it draughty inside and made it look like the kind of shabby hut the French might use as a lavatory, but the Renault 4 was quirky, friendly and endearing. It was the kind of car you might have cried over when your Dad came to sell it.

YEARS MADE 1961–93
TOP SPEED 82mph (1100)
0–60MPH ACCELERATION 18.2 sec (1100)
MAXIMUM POWER 34bhp (1100)
BEST OVERALL FUEL ECONOMY 43mpg (750)
ORIGINAL PRICE £549 (750 in 1962)
POP FACT The Renault 4 is the fifth best-selling car of all time, with 8,135,422 sold between 1961 and 1993. It's beaten only by (in order of sales prowess) the VW Beetle, Fiat 124/Lada, Ford Model T and Fiat Uno.

107

MINI

(1959–2000)

We've all got the Mini story pretty much off pat. It goes something like: born in 1959, radical front-wheel-drive design, seems a bit weird at first, then becomes '60s style icon and celebrity favourite, evolves into a rally hero then '70s fuel-crisis survivor until it pops out into the '80s under the shadow of new big brother Metro. Starts to fade into the background only to be reinvented as groovy bonnet-striped retro novelty item in the '90s before quietly passing away in favour of equally groovy but conspicuously not 'mini' new Mini, which is very cute but actually a BMW.

But that's to overlook the core of this car's life. Most Minis weren't owned by Peter Sellers or driven by rally drivers, or even, as more recently, seized upon by hepcat urbanites who wanted a cool old-skool car with a white roof. No, back in the days when the Mini wasn't the funkster we all remember, it was a simple, functional family car.

Nowadays a family won't travel unless their massive MPV has seat belts for all and enough air bags to start a balloon festival. Yet there was a time when the whole clan, and perhaps a couple of other families' kids, would squidge

YEARS MADE 1959–2000

TOP SPEED 100mph
(1275cc Cooper Si, 1992)

0–60MPH ACCELERATION 7.6 sec
(1275cc Mini Cooper S carburettor, 1990)

MAXIMUM POWER 76bhp
(1275cc Cooper S Mk 1, 1964)

BEST OVERALL FUEL ECONOMY
40mpg (850cc Austin Mini Se7en/
Morris Mini Minor Mk 1)

ORIGINAL PRICE £497
(Austin Se7en/Morris in 1959)

POP FACT In 1960, only 116,000 Minis were sold because the public was still wary of it. Worse still, Ford bought a Mini, dismantled it, and calculated – rightly – that BMC was selling the car at a loss.

into a Mini and head off for a day out. For this ability, the little Mini was often called a miracle of packaging, but the real packaging genius was your Dad, who managed to get everyone in there without sawing off a few legs. They didn't even fit rear seat belts in those days, and the nearest you'd get to an air bag was hiding behind your fat brother. Best of all, no one knew any better and the Mini, with its jaunty, bouncy suspension and permanently whining gearbox seemed like a rather jolly way to get around. Of course, if Dad were really worried about a call from the child-cruelty people, perhaps he'd have splashed out on the more spacious Traveller-estate version, and if he were feeling really lavish he could even order it with twee wood trim stuck to the outside.

But whatever model Dad chose, the Mini was a stout foot soldier of family life and that didn't make it any less heroic than its relatives zipping past Carnaby Street or monstering the Monte Carlo rally. The saddest thing about the Mini is that it did 41 years of sterling service for Britain and yet it seems to have disappeared. It used to be a fixture on any street in any town; now you barely see one at all. Like the long, hot summers of your childhood, it's sad how something great so quickly becomes just a memory.

9 SPORTY DAD

He still loved you, even if he was trying to pretend he didn't have kids at all.

OPEL MANTA
(1970–1988)

At first glance you might think this was a mundane Vauxhall Cavalier coming towards you. And at first glance you might also think it was a normal Dad behind the wheel.

But haaang on a second. Lower roofline? Only two doors? We're dealing with something, and someone, a bit special here. In truth the Manta really was just a low-slung Cavalier, the sporty body disguising functional oily bits that made it somewhat less than Ferrari-ish to drive. But then your Dad was likewise still your Dad, and having a faintly groovy car didn't stop him also being the person who would tell you off for walking muddy shoes across the sitting-room carpet. As such, Manta and Dad went together perfectly as an equal melding of excitement and sensibleness. In idle moments he could read news stories about the glamorous and successful Manta rally cars – yes, HIS car was a rally car – but at the same time he was safe in the knowledge that the moderately useful rear seats meant he could still cram the kids back there, staving off having to buy a boring saloon car for at least another year.

YEARS MADE 1970–75 (Mk 1), 1975–88 (Mk 2, shown)
TOP SPEED 121mph (Mk 2 2-litre GT/E)
0–60MPH ACCELERATION 8.5 sec (Mk 2 2-litre GT/E)
MAXIMUM POWER 110bhp (Mk 2 2-litre GT/E)
BEST OVERALL FUEL ECONOMY 26mpg (1600 Mk 1)
ORIGINAL PRICE £1327 (1600 Mk 1 in 1970)
POP FACT A special version of the Manta Mk 1, available through Britain's Opel dealers, was one of the first turbocharged cars to be sold in the UK.

115

FORD CAPRI

(1969–1987)

The Capri became a laughing stock right around the time that Essex-girl jokes hit their misogynist zenith, but let's not forget what this car represented in better days. It may have been little more than a load of saloon-car gubbins in a coupé body, but what a body it was. And the genius of the Capri actually was the use of those everyday mechanical parts because they made it affordable, cheap to run and easy to fix. In other words, they meant your Dad could have a sporty, or sporty-ish, car without having to cancel Christmas.

The sportiness, or sporty-ishness, of his Capri very much depended on which engine he chose. The 2-litre ones were pretty brisk, the 1.6 a bit less so, the 1.3 couldn't pull over a newborn giraffe. But these engines were the mere bread and butter. What Dad wanted, and if you were really lucky what he could afford, was the Capri 3-litre. Put it this way, TV crime fighters *The Professionals* didn't mince about in a 1300cc Capri. They blazed everywhere behind three whole litres of V6 power, because they were MEN! Yes! In the late '70s it was hard to conceive of a car that was as exciting and yet tantalizingly attainable as the Ford Capri 3.0S. At least until 1981 when Ford binned the 3-litre and replaced it with

YEARS MADE 1969–74 (Mark I), 1974–8 (Mk 2, shown), 1978–87 (Mk 3)
TOP SPEED 127mph (Mk 3 2.8i)
0–60MPH ACCELERATION 7.9 sec (Mk 3 2.8i)
MAXIMUM POWER 160bhp (Mk 3 2.8i)
BEST OVERALL FUEL ECONOMY 26mpg (Mk 1 1300GT)
ORIGINAL PRICE £1088 (2-litre GT in 1970)
POP FACT Ford really did want the Capri to be the European Mustang. They were even going to call it Colt until they discovered Mitsubishi already owned the name.

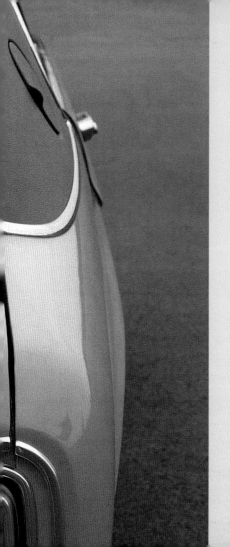

the 2.8i. That little 'i' after the name was important because it meant Ford had chucked away old-fashioned carburettors and embraced the buzz of '80s technology with something called fuel injection. There were even little 'injection' stickers on the front wings to remind you. You didn't actually know what injection was, but that was hardly important. It just sounded exciting and powerful, just as the Capri 2.8i looked exciting and powerful with its glaring headlamps and fat alloy wheels.

Sadly, that was the peak for the Capri, after which it started to look like a '70s throwback. Even your Dad had chucked away his flares and cheesecloth shirts by the mid-'80s, but here was the poor old Capri, soldiering on in British showrooms until 1986, two years after it was killed off in the rest of Europe. The UK really did love the Capri because for us it was the British Ford Mustang. Although only in the same way that Cliff Richard is the British Elvis.

RELIANT SCIMITAR GTE

(1968–1986)

For sheer jump-around-and-do-a-little-wee-in-your-pants childhood excitement, the Scimitar GTE was a formidable bit of kit. For starters it was rare, which meant there was little chance of another Dad turning up to school in one, and of course it had those fabulous coupé-cum-estate looks that were quite unlike anything else. Except maybe the Volvo P1800ES, but that came out a good four years after the GTE, so nurrr. For Dad it wasn't all about style and a stout Ford V6 either because there was also a moderate amount of room in the back for kids and the body was rust-proof glassfibre. Yes, the GTE truly was sensible but exciting. A bit too exciting if you counted its habit of sometimes catching fire.

In its '70s heyday the Scimitar enjoyed several celebrity owners including badger-esque sports anchor Dickie Davies, perma-chuckling *It's a Knockout* gaffer Stuart Hall and, most famously, Princess Anne who was given a GTE as a twentieth-birthday present and owned a succession of them thereafter. In 1976 she was stopped for speeding in her Scimitar, but let off by the policeman who was erroneously impressed to find a horse that could drive a car. Actually, that last bit's a complete fib.

YEARS MADE 1968–75 (SE5 or Mk 1), 1975–86 (SE6/SE6b or Mk 2)
TOP SPEED 122mph (SE6b)
0–60MPH ACCELERATION 8.8 sec (SE6b)
MAXIMUM POWER 172bhp (SE5/SE6)
BEST OVERALL FUEL ECONOMY 24mpg (SE6b)
ORIGINAL PRICE £1759 (SE5 in 1969)
POP FACT The Scimitar GTE was styled by a man called Tom Karen who also takes credit for another '70s icon: the Raleigh Chopper bike.

TRIUMPH STAG

(1970–1977)

This was the impossibly glamorous peak of Sporty Dadness. If your Dad had a Stag it didn't just mean he was doing rather well for himself; it also suggested that he was sophisticated and caddish, more suited to swishing along the Côte d'Azur than popping down the road to buy a paper. Such was the Stag's air of carefree grooviness that whenever your mother was in the car it was almost mandatory for her to wear a head scarf. Meanwhile, the kids could squash into the tiny back seats and enjoy the thrill of being beaten half to death by the rush of wind as Dad summoned up his mighty V8 power.

Of course, 'mighty' wasn't a word you would apply to the general construction of that 3-litre engine. In fact, 'downright shoddy' would have been more accurate because the Stag's motor was famous for going wrong, most notably by boiling over like an unattended pot. But when the Stag worked it was magnificent. Where the engines in normal Dad cars wheezed and rattled, the Stag's V8 burbled and roared. It was like Tom Jones singing in the middle of the school choir. Knowing your Dad had a Stag was second only to discovering that he'd just got a job as a secret agent.

YEARS MADE 1970–77
TOP SPEED 118mph
0–60MPH ACCELERATION 9.7 sec
MAXIMUM POWER 145bhp
BEST OVERALL FUEL ECONOMY 22mpg
ORIGINAL PRICE £2441 (in 1970)
POP FACT The Stag was the first sporty Triumph not to feature an old-fashioned separate chassis – it used the floorpan of the 2000 saloon. That distinctive T-bar above the front seats was there to stop the whole structure going floppy once the bracing benefits of a normal roof had been removed.

23

PRACTICAL DAD

The Dad who needs to carry a lot of stuff.

PEUGEOT 504 ESTATE
(1971–1982)

Entire African nations have been founded on the 504 estate, so family life was never going to be much of a struggle. This was a Peugeot from the old school, as tough as an elephant in a flak vest, making it less a car, more the kind of thing that might be handed down through generations, assuming later ones could weld the rusty bits. The 504's trump card was its vast interior, which really came into its own if Dad had bought the Family model with a third row of seats in the Albert Hall-sized boot. Never mind his family, he could invite along a couple of other families if he felt like it, and they could all bounce along on those cheekily ribbed seats.

Not long ago Peugeot started selling an estate with three rows of seats again, but it was based on the poky 307 hatchback and as such wasn't fit to lick the wheels of this old warhorse. They really don't build them like this any more. Except, actually they do, because in some African countries you can still buy a brand-new 504. That's how much they still love it. About as much, in fact, as everyone loved the big, amiable family bus that meant you could always invite your friends along. And their friends. And their friends' friends. And their friends' friends' friends. And …

YEARS MADE 1971–82

TOP SPEED 95mph (2-litre)

0–60MPH ACCELERATION 14.1 sec (2-litre)

MAXIMUM POWER 93bhp (2-litre)

BEST OVERALL FUEL ECONOMY 30mpg (2.3-litre diesel)

ORIGINAL PRICE £1795 (2-litre petrol in 1972)

POP FACT The Peugeot 504 may have been Car of the Year in 1969 but it also holds the dubious honour of being the vehicle in which Mark Thatcher got lost in the Sahara Desert during the 1982 Paris–Dakar Rally.

127

VOLVO 245

(1974–1993)

Short of putting your family in an actual tank, there was no better way to feel the warm glow of keeping them safe than installing them in the tank-like Volvo 245. Years before other car-makers realized that safety was a selling point, Volvo were proud to describe how they carefully designed each new model and then ruthlessly slung it at a concrete block to test its strength. And usually it was the concrete block that got broken. This was terrifically reassuring for the Volvo-driving Dad, the relentless ticking of the 'fasten seat belt' monitor every morning like a reassuring heartbeat of bosomy concern and love for his kids.

More than that, the 245 was a rubber-bumpered totem of stout middle-class values. In fact, it should have come as standard with the little GB sticker on the back, just so the world knew you took your holidays in France, not crammed into some nasty Dan Air flight to the Med. Best of all, because the Volvo had the kind of luggage space only a van could match, it would swallow the family's holiday gubbins with plenty of room left over for a case or two of that delicious Bordeaux. All transported back across the Channel in complete and utter safety.

YEARS MADE 1974–93

TOP SPEED 105mph (2.3-litre)

0–60MPH ACCELERATION 10.1 sec (2.3-litre)

MAXIMUM POWER 112bhp (2.3-litre)

BEST OVERALL FUEL ECONOMY 26mpg (2-litre)

ORIGINAL PRICE £3099 (245DL in 1975)

POP FACT This car quickly gained a following in suburban Britain. Hence, a yellow 245 was perfectly cast as Jerry Leadbetter's car in '70s Surbiton sit-com *The Good Life*.

129

LAND-ROVER
(1948–1985)

If Dad's car has a Land-Rover badge on the front these days it doesn't necessarily mean he's going to use it for anything more strenuous than bouncing over speed bumps. But there was a time when Land-Rover didn't mean a preened fashion statement for looking down on other commuters. It meant THE Land-Rover, a rough, tough working machine that could be driven through ditches and repaired with a hammer.

The Land-Rover was simple as a spade and just as effective. It wasn't about posing – how could you show off in something that resembled a collapsing shed? – it was about getting the job done. Chances are if Dad had one his job was farming, and the Land-Rover was his slightly scruffy ally, like a border collie on knobbly tyres. And, of course, if you lived on a farm, that meant plenty of land on which Dad might one day let you loose to make those first tentative lurches towards your driving licence. Or at least being allowed to drive the tractor across to the far field.

It was heavy to drive, it was mucky, it almost certainly smelt a bit. But it got the job done like no modern Freelander. For one thing, *they* have carpets and power steering. Wusses.

YEARS MADE 1948–57 (Series I, shown), 1957–71 (Series II), 1971–85 (Series III)
TOP SPEED 84mph (Series III V8 LWB)
0–60MPH ACCELERATION 16.9 sec (Series III V8 LWB)
MAXIMUM POWER 93bhp (Series III V8)
BEST OVERALL FUEL ECONOMY 21mpg (Series I 2-litre petrol)
ORIGINAL PRICE £450 (Series I in 1948)
POP FACT When they were sketching out the Land-Rover back in the 1940s, the designers seriously considered putting the steering wheel in the middle to save having to engineer it for both left- and right-hand drive.

3

FORD TRANSIT

(1965–1985)

You know you've really made it when your brand name becomes the everyday word for something. Vacuums are Hoovers. Ballpoint pens are Biros. And for near-on four decades, vans are Transits. With good cause too, because the Transit was the start of a new era, using car suspension, steering and brakes so that it drove more like a car and less like 1930s farm machinery. Little wonder that British criminals of the '60s started ditching their Jags in favour of this radical van whenever they had, erm, 'jobs' to do because the Transit was far less conspicuous yet still had the speed and handling they needed to make a fast getaway.

Even if your Dad didn't do a bank job that involved wearing tights on his head, he'd still appreciate that the Transit was one of the most versatile and accommodating vans ever made. For him it was a tool of the trade, but for kids it was just brilliant fun. With no back seats you had the honour of riding shotgun while children in cars were still relegated to row two, and in a time before urban 4×4s you were looking down on all of them. It didn't matter that the Transit was rattly and noisy and the interior was filthy. Sitting up high next to your Dad at the wheel made you feel king of the world.

YEARS MADE 1965–78 (original shape, shown), 1978–85 ('new shape')

TOP SPEED 90mph estimated ('new shape' 3-litre V6 van)

0–60MPH ACCELERATION data not available

MAXIMUM POWER 136bhp ('new shape' 3-litre V6)

BEST OVERALL FUEL ECONOMY data not available

ORIGINAL PRICE £542 (1.7-litre V4 petrol van in 1965)

POP FACT Ford of Europe was created in 1965 but the Transit holds the distinction of being the very first Ford vehicle jointly developed by Ford's then separate British and German operations.

133

TOYOTA SPACE CRUISER
(1983–1990)

Renault always takes the credit in Europe for inventing the MPV. In fact, before their Espace people carrier arrived Toyota had already come up with their own practical, if slightly weird interpretation of the same idea. But there's one good reason why it's the French that get the glory. The Espace was the first MPV designed as such from scratch, whereas the Space Cruiser was just a van with windows.

Still, at the time it seemed novel, what with its high mounted flipping and folding seats. Plus, you got in and out of the back through a sliding door, so you could almost pretend you were in *The A-Team*. Except the A-Team's van wasn't available in garish two-tone paint, nor was it entirely upholstered in tacky velour-like fabrics. Still, it seemed cool at the time. Not so cool for Dad behind the wheel because the Space Cruiser wasn't a quick machine nor – as Dad-tastic consumer bible *Which?* magazine proved during testing – was it especially stable, being prone to almost smacking its jutting chin on the ground under hard braking. Which just proved that while the Space Cruiser was undoubtedly practical and slightly amusing for kids, it was also a bit of a lash-up.

YEARS MADE 1983–90

TOP SPEED 91mph (2-litre)

0–60MPH ACCELERATION 16.2 sec (2-litre)

MAXIMUM POWER 87bhp (2-litre)

BEST OVERALL FUEL ECONOMY 23mpg (1.8-litre)

ORIGINAL PRICE £7981 (1.8-litre in 1983)

POP FACT The van on which the Space Cruiser was based was inexplicably called the Lite-Ace.

35

TECHNO DAD

The Dad who appreciated a bit of sophistication.

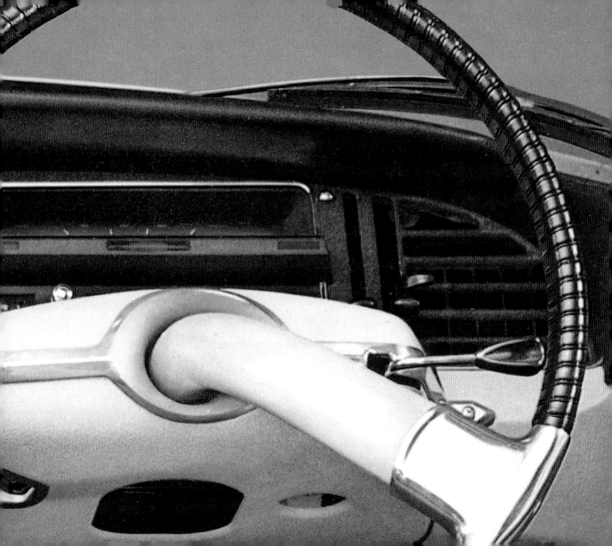

CITROËN DS
(1955–1975)

If your Dad had walked in one day and announced that the entire family were moving to the moon it couldn't have been any more exciting than if he'd arrived home in a Citroën DS. This car wasn't just technically advanced, it was simply on another level compared to any other car in the world. It had hydropneumatic suspension, powered brakes, power steering and a semi-automatic gearbox, and it came with all this in 1955. Imagine the stir this extraordinary-looking car created in a black-and-white world of demob suits and starchy saloons. It took not years but decades for other car-makers to get close, and even when they did the DS still looked radical and beautiful.

The DS is an icon. Its sharky nose, its swooping tail, the cool details like indicators in little pods on either side of the back window and the delicate single-spoke steering wheel, all of these things made it unique. If aliens were monitoring earth during the mid-'50s, scoffing at our lame technology and preparing for a sinister invasion, the arrival of the DS would have been the moment they'd have thought, Oh, no! These people are cleverer than we thought, then scrapped the plan and gone to build a leisure centre on Neptune instead.

YEARS MADE 1955–75

TOP SPEED 120mph (DS23)

0–60MPH ACCELERATION 10.4 sec (DS23)

MAXIMUM POWER 130bhp (DS23)

BEST OVERALL FUEL ECONOMY 26mpg (ID19)

ORIGINAL PRICE £1726 (DS19 in 1956)

POP FACT In 1962 the DS was credited with saving the life of French president General Charles de Gaulle. When a hail of terrorist bullets shot out some of the tyres, his DS's hydropneumatic suspension could compensate for this lopsidedness, enabling his driver to make good an escape.

139

AUSTIN PRINCESS
(1975–1982)

The 1970s is seen as the darkest hour of the British car industry. In the '50s and '60s it bestrode the globe; by the '70s it all went wrong in a blaze of shabby quality and industrial unrest. But look on the bright side: without the '70s we wouldn't have had fabulous curios like the Princess. Because only the unusual decision-making and end-of-the-empire arrogance of 1970s BL could call a meeting and say, 'Hey, let's make a car that looks like a big piece of cheese.'

So, a brave car, but also one with real merit. In particular, it was supremely comfortable, with Dad relaxing into his big, velvety driving seat up front while the kids bounced around on the massive, squishy bench in the back. And that unusual styling grew on you after a while, to the extent that people got used to it and the Princess went from futuristic techno car to almost part of the scenery. The final lurch into normality came when one starred as Terry's car in the uber-normal early '80s sitcom *Terry & June*. Although, if the credit sequence were to be believed, Terry was a man who sometimes put beefburgers on a record player, so behind the suburban façade he was clearly a bit unusual. Just like your Dad in his Princess.

YEARS MADE 1975–82

TOP SPEED 104mph (2.2-litre)

0–60MPH ACCELERATION 13.5 sec (2.2-litre)

MAXIMUM POWER 110bhp (2.2-litre)

BEST OVERALL FUEL ECONOMY 29mpg (1.7-litre)

ORIGINAL PRICE £2117 (Austin 1800 in 1975)

POP FACT This car was launched under three marque names – you could have it as an Austin, a Morris or a Wolseley (shown) – but after just nine months the whole strategy was abandoned and a new marque, Princess, was created for all of them.

NSU Ro80

(1967–1976)

The NSU Ro80 was the ultimate Techno Dad car of its day. Aside from the futuristic styling, the Ro80 was packed with cutting-edge stuff that was almost unheard of in late '60s saloons, including fully independent suspension, all-round disc brakes, power steering and a semi-automatic gearbox. This was about as advanced as you could get, unless your Dad went to work in an actual spaceship. And frankly, even that would have been only slightly more exciting than this.

But the Ro80's real talking point was its Wankel engine – you boy, stop sniggering – which shunned conventional pistons in favour of a rotary design that promised compact dimensions and uncanny smoothness. Which it did, but only alongside a distressing appetite for petrol and oil. In fact, as drink problems go, the Ro80 made Oliver Reed look like a Methodist. Then, as the miles rolled on, crucial seals inside wore out and it was back to the garage for a new engine – again. This was of no small inconvenience to Dad – it might even explain why he went so bald around the same time – but it didn't matter to the kids. All they knew was that Dad drove one of the most sophisticated, unusual and downright groovy cars the world had ever seen.

YEARS MADE 1967–76
TOP SPEED 110mph
0–60MPH ACCELERATION 13.1 sec
MAXIMUM POWER 115bhp
BEST OVERALL FUEL ECONOMY 15mpg
ORIGINAL PRICE £2249 (in 1968)
POP FACT Developing the Wankel engine and then replacing lots of them under warranty was bad for NSU's coffers and it was swallowed by VW in 1969. The NSU factory still exists, but today it builds Audis.

AUDI 100

(1 9 8 3 – 1 9 9 1)

During the '70s most West German saloons were as upright and sturdy as their country's ladies shotputting team. They were also about as sexy. That was until 1983 when Audi belatedly discovered something called 'aerodynamics' and introduced the handsome 100 with a sleek, cigar-shaped body that sliced through the air like a greasy eel. In fact, Audi were so proud of their slippery shape they gummed a little sticker in the side windows bearing the mysterious slogan 'cd 0.30', a reference to the car's drag factor if you stuck it in a wind tunnel. Lacking a wind tunnel of his own, your Dad simply stuck it on the drive as a conspicuous sign that he was embracing the high-tech '80s.

Since aerodynamics don't matter on the inside of cars, the dashboard was rather less sleek – in fact it looked like a matt-black cliff-face – but everything operated with precision, right down to those flush-fitting windows, which on posher models worked electrically with a sort of cool *Star Trek*-ish swish noise. The Audi 100 was one of the first signs of the brave new world of aerodynamics. Although male-pattern baldness meant your Dad had been getting more aerodynamic for years.

YEARS MADE 1983–91

TOP SPEED 134mph (2.2 turbo)

0–60MPH ACCELERATION 7.5 sec (2.2-litre turbo)

MAXIMUM POWER 165bhp (2.2-litre turbo)

BEST OVERALL FUEL ECONOMY 30mpg (100TD)

ORIGINAL PRICE £8772 (1.8-litre in 1984)

POP FACT Audi was so keen to keep the 100's radical shape secret, prototype testing was done largely at night. For added security it fitted test cars with a device to detect camera flash bulbs and instantly fire off another flashlight attached to the car so any plucky spy would find his photos uselessly overexposed.

145

CITROËN GS

(1970–1979)

Medium-sized family cars of the early 1970s were not, in general, an exciting bunch. But you could always rely on the nutjobs from Citroën to arrive at the party wearing a pair of antlers with two lamb chops glued to their face. And that's what happened with the GS back in 1970. Futuristic styling? Check. Complicated hydropneumatic suspension? Check. Weird flat-four engine? Check.

But this wasn't being bonkers for the sake of it. That sleek shape made it aerodynamic, the clever suspension made it comfortable and that unusual engine made it sound unique and interesting in a world of grinding Fords and Vauxhalls. Of course, the boingy suspension could also make you carsick, but at least your family stood out from the crowd as you trundled along wretching into a Woolies bag.

In 1979 the GS was renamed GSA and given a hatchback instead of a normal boot. In this respect it was more conventional; in every other way it was still as mad as a packet of badgers, and now featured a built-in magnifying glass over the speedo so it was easier to read. And that was the Citroën GS all over: slightly weird, but also rather clever.

YEARS MADE 1970–79

TOP SPEED 94mph (1.2-litre)

0–60MPH ACCELERATION 14.9 sec (1.2-litre)

MAXIMUM POWER 60bhp (1.2-litre)

BEST OVERALL FUEL ECONOMY 26mpg (1.0-litre)

ORIGINAL PRICE £1001 (GS Club 1.0-litre in 1970)

POP FACT The GS's looks owed much to a late '60s concept car called the 1100 Berlina Aerodinamica, built for British Leyland by Italian designer Pininfarina. BL decided not to use the design and instead came up with the Austin Allegro. Great.

147

12 CORTINA DAD

The very definition of the Dad car.

FORD CORTINA MK 1
(1962–1966)

The Ford Cortina provided 20 years of sterling service as the bastion of Dadness, and it all started here. The formula was simple, based around straightforward engineering. But that was no accident because it made the Cortina affordable and Ford's real skill was dressing it in a desirable body that looked like an American car of the late '50s run through a filter of British modesty.

There was even a sporty GT model, packing twin carbs and enough exciting add-ons to make Dad drool into his milky tea. Even with just 78bhp, the Cortina GT was brisk enough to let him pretend he was Graham Hill. Unless, of course, your Dad actually was Graham Hill, in which case he'd have a Lotus Cortina, an exotic snorter with lightweight aluminium panels, 1.6-litre twin-cam engine and a dashing green stripe down the side. But while the Lotus Cortina covered itself in race glory, its ordinary brothers were doing more important things: taking people to work, carting the family around at weekends, quietly getting on with the vital business of mobilizing whole swathes of Britain. The Cortina was a solid fixture of life, comforting and reassuring in its familiarity, just like your Dad himself.

YEARS MADE 1962–6

TOP SPEED* 91mph (GT)

0–60MPH ACCELERATION* 12.1 sec (GT)

MAXIMUM POWER* 83.5bhp (GT)

BEST OVERALL FUEL ECONOMY 30mpg (Cortina De Luxe 1.2-litre)

ORIGINAL PRICE £666 (Cortina De Luxe 1.2-litre in 1962)

POP FACT During development, the Mk 1 Cortina was code-named 'Archbishop'. This was Ford UK's riposte to Ford Germany, which was developing its own medium-sized car, code-named 'Cardinal'. The British thought an archbishop outranked a cardinal, although they later discovered it's the reverse.

* The Lotus Cortina Mk 1 offered 108mph, 0–60mph in 9.9 sec, and 105bhp, but few Dads were ready for that sort of heady power.

FORD CORTINA MK 2
(1966–1970)

People worked hard in the 1960s. Modern bands turn out an album every two or three years. The Beatles could record two LPs inside 12 months. And where modern cars last for six or seven years, Ford came up with a new Cortina after just four. This wasn't simply a diligent work ethic of course; the original 'Tina had been a huge success but these were fast-changing times and Ford had to make sure its super-popular Dad car didn't become old hat. So, they threw away the pretty Mk 1 body to replace it with a more sober suit that sat on the original's chassis but looked brand new, and went on to peg another seven-figure sales total. Ching!

The Mk 2 stuck with the original's range of models, including a racy GT and very racy Lotus Cortina but introduced a new version to sit between the two. It was called the 1600E and it was the stuff of Cortina legend. The constituent parts were nothing new – it was basically a GT with Lotus Cortina suspension and a poshed-up interior – but as a whole it was enough to make your Dad fumble for the savings book. And that was the Ford Cortina all over. Like pork chops and mash served off Twiggy's belly, it was basic, honest fare set alight by superb presentation.

YEARS MADE 1966–70

TOP SPEED* 98mph (1600E)

0–60MPH ACCELERATION* 13.1 sec (1600E)

MAXIMUM POWER* 88bhp (1600E)

BEST OVERALL FUEL ECONOMY 27mpg (1300)

ORIGINAL PRICE £791 (1600 four-door de luxe in 1968)

POP FACT The Mk 2's body was actually less rigid than the Mk 1's, as rally drivers discovered when hard driving made their new Lotus Cortinas go banana shaped.

* The Cortina Lotus Mk 2 offered 106mph, 0–60mph in 9.9 sec and 109bhp but few Dads were that flash with their cash.

53

FORD CORTINA MK 3

(1970–1976)

After the sweet Mk 1 and plain Jane Mk 2, the Mk 3 was where the Cortina really sexed up to become quite the '70s glamour puss. Just look at the smooth curves, the deep-set grille and those fulsome hips. Phwoar. The design influence came from America, but the end result was resolutely and buxomly British. Sort of like Diana Dors with chrome bumpers. The mechanical parts remained as simple as steak and chips, but the trimmings made it alluring, especially when Ford invented a successor to the Mk 2's much loved 1600E, now called the 2000E because it had a 2-litre engine as well as a wooden dash and so much velour you couldn't have got more '70s if the seats had been embossed with images of Slade on a Raleigh Chopper.

The Mk 3 may have lost the exciting Lotus version of the previous two generations, but with the 2000E lesser Cortina owners still had something to aspire to. Plus, of course, the 1970s Cortina was little brother to the hard man Granada that served *The Sweeney* so well. Which meant that Dad could indulge a quiet fantasy of squealing the tyres and shouting, 'SHUT IT!', even if he were just on his way to collect your Mum from her mother's.

YEARS MADE 1970–76

TOP SPEED 105mph (2-litre)

0–60MPH ACCELERATION 10.7 sec (2-litre)

MAXIMUM POWER 98bhp (2-litre)

BEST OVERALL FUEL ECONOMY 23.5mpg (1.3-litre)

ORIGINAL PRICE £914 (1300 in 1970)

POP FACT The Cortina Mk 3 was the first car to use combinations of letters instead of names to denote trim levels, ranging from L, through XL and GT, up to GXL. Almost every mainstream car range copied this template for the next two decades.

155

FORD CORTINA MK 4/5
(1976–1982)

By the time the Ford Cortina entered the fourth phase of its life it was an easy synonym for average, normal, run of the mill. Maybe Ford didn't help matters because, after the hips-'n'-lips Mk 3 version, the Mk 4 looked like a sort of child's drawing of a car: just a big box with two smaller boxes stuck to either end.

Yet despite the disparaging way in which the word 'Cortina' could be used, this car was a totem of British life. Whatever you did, wherever you went, you might barely notice it but there was the Cortina, getting on with business. Cortinas carrying stressed reps to meetings 200 miles away. Cortinas ferrying excitable kids to the swimming baths. Cortinas carting miserable kids to a weekend at grandma's. Cortina estates engaged in none-more-Dadish tasks than taking sacks of rubbish to the tip. Cortinas in car parks late at night acting as an impromptu love nest with a vinyl roof. Any time, any place, there was a Cortina, playing its part in British life. And the Mk 4 carried on that stout lineage with the same effective formula that had made Cortinas 1 to 3 so successful. Mechanical bits as complex as a pair of scissors, body that blended perfectly into the scenery

YEARS MADE 1976–82

TOP SPEED 103mph (2-litre)

0–60MPH ACCELERATION 10.3 sec (2-litre)

MAXIMUM POWER 102bhp (2-litre)

BEST OVERALL FUEL ECONOMY 32mpg (1.3-litre)

ORIGINAL PRICE £2548 (1600GL in 1976)

POP FACT The Cortina is named after an Italian town, Cortina d'Ampezzo, which was the scene of the 1956 Winter Olympics. However, it doesn't sound so exotic in Italian, where the Ford Cortina literally translates as the Ford Curtain. By the way, the 1980 Mk 5 Cortina was merely a lightly revised Mk 4.

157

of the times, clever trimming to make it seem appealing while keeping the whole shebang affordable and sensible.

But the Cortina's time was almost up. One last serious revamp – sometimes called the Mk 5 – in 1980 retained the same shape but fiddled with the details, and managed to keep it at the top of the sales charts. Truth is, it was a holding operation because the old dear was getting aged and creaky until, in 1982, the Cortina passed away.

In the cleaner, brighter, whiter '80s people wanted more sophistication from their cars and it was down to the radical new Ford Sierra to provide it. The simple old Cortina, the car that had kept a million Dads on the road, it just wasn't enough any more. But, as the very heart of the Dad car and everything that stands for, it had more than done its job.

159

**For Peter Chapman (Giles's Dad)
and Phil Porter (Richard's Dad).**

20 19 18 17 16 15 14 13 12 11

Published in 2007 by BBC Books, an imprint of Ebury Publishing

Ebury Publishing is a division of the Random House Group

Copyright © Giles Chapman and Richard Porter 2007

Giles Chapman and Richard Porter have asserted their right to be identified as the authors of this Work in accordance with the Copyright, Designs and Patents Act 1988.

The Random House Group Limited Reg. No. 954009

Addresses for companies within the Random House Group can be found at www.randomhouse.co.uk

A CIP catalogue record for this book is available from the British Library

ISBN 978 0 563 53919 3

The Random House Group Limited makes every effort to ensure that the papers used in our books are made from trees that have been legally sourced from well-managed and credibly certified forests. Our paper procurement policy can be found at www.randomhouse.co.uk

Commissioning editor: Shirley Patton
Project editor: Christopher Tinker
Copy-editor: Tessa Clark
Design: Smith & Gilmour
Production controller: Kenneth McKay

Printed and bound in Italy by Printer Trento Srl
Colour origination by Dot Gradations, Wickford, Essex

*The opinions expressed in this book are those of the authors
and do not necessarily reflect those of Top Gear or BBC Books.*

Picture credits

*BBC Books would like to thank the following for
providing photographs and for permission to
reproduce copyright material. While every effort
has been made to trace and acknowledge
copyright holders, we would like to apologize
should there be any errors or omissions.*

Giles Chapman Library: pp. 2, 8–9, 16, 22, 24, 26–7, 30, 34, 40, 44, 46, 50–1, 56, 62–3, 66, 70, 74–5, 80, 86–7, 88, 94, 100, 116, 124–5, 128, 130, 132, 134, 140, 144 and 152.

LAT Photographic: pp. 10, 12–13, 28, 64, 68, 90, 92, 110–11, 114, 118–19, 126, 142, 156 and 158.

Photographs on the following pages are reproduced from original sales brochures stocked by Pooks Motor Books of Rothley, Leicestershire (Tel. 0116 237 6222; e-mail pooks.motorbooks@virgin.net): pp. 6, 14, 18, 20, 32, 36–7, 38, 42, 48, 52, 54, 58, 60, 72, 76, 78, 82, 84, 96, 98–9, 102, 104, 106, 108, 112–13, 120, 122, 136–7, 138, 146, 148–9, 150 and 154.

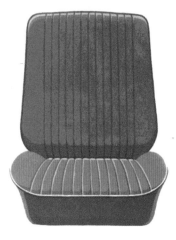